VIDEO & AUDIO INCLUDED 

CREATIVE ACTIVITIES

FOR TEACHING GENERAL MUSIC

BY VICTORIA BOLER

To access video and audio, visit:
www.halleonard.com/mylibrary

Enter Code
1230-9818-5660-5848

Doña Araña (page 7) and Duerme Pronto (page 46) are from *Vamos a cantar: 230 Latino and Hispanic Folk Songs to Sing, Read, and Play* (edited by Faith Knowles). Used with permission from The Kodály Institute at Capital University.

ISBN 978-1-70515-150-1

Visit Hal Leonard Online at
www.halleonard.com

World headquarters, contact:
Hal Leonard
7777 West Bluemound Road
Milwaukee, WI 53213
Email: info@halleonard.com

In Europe, contact:
Hal Leonard Europe Limited
1 Red Place
London, W1K 6PL
Email: info@halleonardeurope.com

In Australia, contact:
Hal Leonard Australia Pty. Ltd.
4 Lentara Court
Cheltenham, Victoria, 3192 Australia
Email: info@halleonard.com.au

USING THIS BOOK

The activities in this book are designed to take between five and twenty minutes to explore. Feel free to repeat lesson segments as necessary, and use as much of the project as is appropriate for your situation.

Creativity and the Curriculum: These learning experiences are intended to be woven into the larger elementary general music curriculum. Rather than teaching improvisation, arranging, and composition as isolated units, students use these creative processes to engage with the curricular sequence on a deeper level.

There are flexible options for notational literacy throughout the book so you can choose the appropriate notation pathway for your situation.

Assessing Creativity: Each lesson segment in this book is accompanied by a quantitative assessment. These objective measurements of student musicianship are imperative to planning future instruction.

However, many more avenues of assessment are utilized in these activities to provide a more holistic picture than quantitative data can measure. Students use self-assessments to think about their musical learning. They use whole-class and small-group assessments to evaluate their progress as an ensemble. The qualitative data you gather throughout the learning process (how students engage in the material, what their creations sound like, how they're working together in their group, etc.) narrate an important story behind the quantitative score.

FRAMING CREATIVITY

In these activities, musical creativity is framed around making musical choices.

As teachers, the parameters we set on those choices impact the name we give the creative process: improvisation, arranging, or composition. For the purposes of this book, *improvisation* is a spontaneous musical choice that exists in the moment. *Arranging* is a musical choice about the re-structure of given elements. Those elements might be provided by the teacher or given in the song. Lastly, a *composition* is a musical choice about original musical ideas. Those ideas are practiced and then preserved through memorization, through teaching it to someone else, through audio, through video, or through notation. With this lens, any artistic choice students make in the classroom is a creative choice because it represents a student's unique musical thought.

Co-Creating the Creative Classroom: There are many levels of partnerships used in these activities. Students are asked to create as individuals, in partnership with friends, in small groups, and as a whole-class ensemble. When we present musical options as a core component of our curriculum, we meet our students as co-creators. Students co-create the *repertoire* as they make musical decisions through improvisation, arranging, and composing. Students co-create the *classroom environment* as they set up a welcoming space where their peers share musical ideas. They co-create the future *learning activities* as they interact with the material and provide information through assessment data about what to do next. They also co-create the music program's role in the *community* by shaping the performances that will be shared outside the classroom.

There are endless possibilities when we look for creative activities for teaching general music. Use these lesson segments as the tip of the iceberg and watch your students imagine many more ideas on their own.

CONTENTS

IMPROVISATION: LOWER ELEMENTARY

Melodic Contour Improvisation: Doña Araña

Translation: *Mrs. Spider went for a stroll. She spun a thread and tried to climb up. Along came the wind that caused her to dance. Along came the rain storm that made her come down.*

Improvisation Project: Melodic contour improvisation

Preparing the Project:

- Before the project, students should be able to sing "Doña Araña" without teacher assistance.
- **Introducing the Song:** Sing the song while performing the fingerplay. Students copy the fingerplay as they listen. *What could this song be about? Why do you think that? Are there any words you recognize?* Repeat the song between each round of questions. Share that this is a song about a spider. *What do you think happened to Mrs. Spider?* Take student suggestions and continue singing the song between each round of answers, with students copying motions. Share that this is a song about Mrs. Spider, who went for a walk. She was trying to spin her web and climb, but then the wind blew and it made her dance! Then the rain came, and she got washed down! Ask students to sing the first phrase: "Doña Araña se fue a pasear." Over the course of several interactions with the song, transition to students singing the whole song without teacher assistance.

CLASS 1

Objective: Students echo melodic contour

Assessment:

The student echoes melodic contour	
4	The student echoes melodic contour with complete pitch accuracy
3	The student echoes melodic contour with near pitch accuracy
2	The student vocalizes the approximate melodic contour without matching pitch
1	The student does not follow the melodic contour, or does not vocalize

Process:

- Sing the song while moving fingers like spiders to act out the story (walk spider fingers on the floor, move fingers up to climb the string, dance in the wind, and come back down with the rain).
- At the end of the song, improvise a vocal exploration while moving spider fingers to match the melodic contour.

- Motion for students to echo the vocal improvisation and movements.
    - **Teaching the Song Gradually:** Notice that students can still engage with the purpose of the activity (melodic contour) before singing the song independently. If this song is new to your students, consider repeating this lesson segment several times with the process for introducing the song. Gradually transition to students singing more phrases of the song without teacher assistance.

CLASS 2

Objective: Students vocalize a melodic contour to match a movement improvisation

Assessment:

The student vocalizes a melodic contour that matches the movement contour of the improvisation	
3	The student vocalizes a melodic contour that matches the movement contour of the improvisation
1	The student vocalizes a melodic contour that does not match the movement contour of the improvisation, or the student does not vocalize

Process:

- Seated in a circle, review previous class: Sing the song while moving fingers like spiders to act out the story (walk spider fingers on the floor, move fingers up to climb the string, dance in the wind, and come back down with the rain).
- Motion for students to stand in the circle.
- Choose one student to stand in the middle of the circle and spin a spider web by moving up, down, and around. The student musicians standing in the circle follow the melodic contour of the spider movements with their voices.
- When the student is done moving, they end their movement improvisation by standing in front of another musician in the circle. That student is the new leader and the vocal exploration continues.
    - **SEL Relationship Skills:** *How will you decide who to choose next for the movement activity? Will you choose your best friend every time? Will you practice what it's like to choose someone you haven't talked to much today?*

CLASS 3

Objective: Students play melodic contour on barred instruments

Assessment:

The student plays melodic contour on a barred instrument	
3	The student plays melodic contour on a barred instrument
1	The student does not play melodic contour on a barred instrument

Materials: Barred instruments (approximately three sets)

Process:

- Sing the song and perform the fingerplay.
- Review previous class: Students stand in a circle. One student in the middle is the spider spinning a web. That student improvises movements up and down. The students standing in the circle follow the melodic contour of the spider movements with their voices.
- Motion for students to sit. Use a barred instrument placed vertically on a chair or other object as a visual. Ask students to help Doña Araña move up and down the instrument by pointing at the bars and vocalizing as you play up, down, and around.

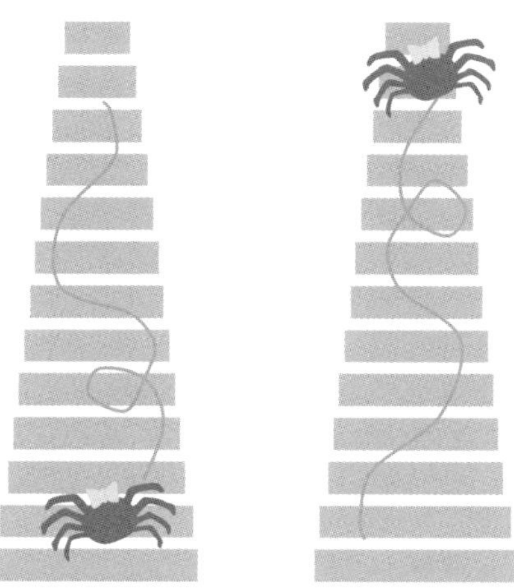

- Ask student volunteers to come to the instrument and share their spider dance on the barred instrument. When the student is done, ask them to hand their mallets to someone else in the circle who is showing they're ready for an instrument.

  Classroom Management and Barred Instruments: It can be helpful to have a "ready to play" signal that students can show, such as a quiet thumbs up. If a student is showing a quiet thumbs up, they are ready to play! If they show a thumbs up while continuing to talk, they are almost ready to play.

- Demonstrate that we can play high and low when the barred instrument is on the floor.

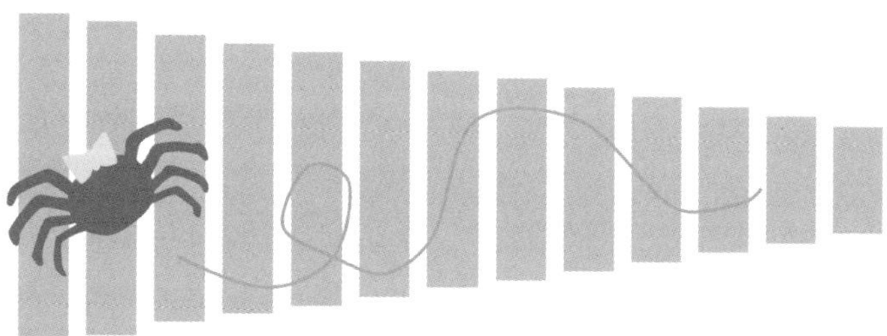

- Place three barred instruments in the middle of the circle. Students take turns exploring sounds on the instruments as the rest of the class improvises a vocal melodic contour. Then students at the instruments hand their mallets to someone, showing they are ready for a turn.

  SEL Self-Management: *It can be so disappointing when we don't get chosen to play an instrument, especially if we really wanted a chance to play! What can we do when we feel disappointed?*

CLASS 4

Objective: Students play melodic contour on barred instruments to match a movement improvisation

Assessment:

The student plays melodic contour on a barred instrument that matches a movement improvisation	
3	The student plays melodic contour on a barred instrument that matches a movement improvisation
1	The student plays melodic contour on a barred instrument that does not match a movement improvisation, or does not play

Materials: Barred instruments (approximately enough for each student to have an instrument, or share an instrument with a partner), scarves (three or four)

Process:

- Choose one student to be the spider and give them a scarf.
- Ask the rest of the class to improvise their own vocal melodic contour as they walk to barred instruments.
  - **Moving to Barred Instruments:** How do you expect student musicians to move to barred instruments? What do you expect them to do when they get there? If moving to barred instruments independently is a new procedure for your young musicians, take time to practice expectations and celebrate student success.
- At barred instruments, students watch the spider build the web by moving up, down, and around. Students at the barred instruments play the melodic contour of the spider on barred instruments.
- Hand scarves to two or three additional students and ask them to stand in front of the barred instruments. Students at the barred instruments each choose one spider to watch and give a thumbs up when they've made their choice.
- As the spiders build their webs in open space by moving up, down, and around, students at the barred instruments play the melodic contour of their chosen spider on barred instruments.
- To switch out movers and instrument players, sing the song again. As student musicians sing, the movers walk to a barred instrument player and hand them their scarf.
  - **Respectful Classroom Management:** Use a visual symbol like a thumbs up or an auditory symbol like tone chimes to signal that the improvisation is over, the spider movers should be still, and the barred instrument players should be in rest position.

Text Improvisation with a Beat and Beat Subdivision: Engine Engine

American Chant

Improvisation Project: Text improvisation with a beat and a beat subdivision

Preparing the Project:

- Before the project, students should have experience with a beat and a beat subdivision. They should also be familiar with the rhyme, "Engine Engine Number Nine."
- **Teaching the Rhyme Through Creative Listening:** Lead students around the room in a single-file line as they listen to the rhyme without speaking. Between repetitions of the rhyme, ask questions: *Where do you think we're going? How many people are in your car on the train? Who are you sitting next to? Where are they going? Are we in a hurry to get there?* Eventually lead students to sit down and pat a steady beat as they listen to the rhyme again. Echo each phrase and eventually transition to students speaking the rhyme without assistance.

CLASS 1

Objective: Students clap the words of "Engine Engine Number Nine"

The student claps the words of "Engine Engine Number Nine"	
4	The student claps the words of "Engine Engine Number Nine" with complete accuracy throughout the entire performance
3	The student claps the words of "Engine Engine Number Nine" with complete accuracy throughout the majority of the performance; some articulations of the rhythm may be slightly ahead or behind the steady beat
2	The student claps the words of "Engine Engine Number Nine" inaccurately
1	The student does not clap the words to "Engine Engine Number Nine"

Process:

- Lead students in stepping a steady beat around a circle while speaking the rhyme.
- *Where do you think our train is going?* Motion for students to brainstorm with their shoulder partner.
- Take a few destination ideas, speaking the rhyme again each time. (*Okay, all aboard to the grocery store! … Great, this time, all aboard to outer space!*)
- After a few rounds, tell students they may travel anywhere they want on the train! Ask students to hold their destination in their heads without sharing out loud. Invite students to clap the rhythm of the words and inner hear the rhyme instead of speaking. Students walk a steady beat while clapping the rhythm.
  - **SEL Self-Management:** *Sometimes we use our voices in music class. Sometimes in music we think things without saying them. We can practice both!*
- Motion for students to sit.

- *Let's take our train across some of the states in The United States. We'll stop in Illinois first. Where should we go next?* Take student answers and choose one to use as a class.
    - Use a map of The United States and explore different state names. Alternatively, feel free to use another place, such as your school name, town name, or state name. At this point in the improvisation process the rhythm does not need to strictly line up with notation for a beat and beat subdivision.
- Add a B section (say 2x): *First we'll stop at Illinois. Then we'll stop at* __(student choice)__.

- A student volunteer chooses the next place to stop. Students speak the rhyme while patting a steady beat, then add the B section with the student choice for the second stop.
    - *First we'll stop at Illinois. Then we'll stop at* __(Texas / Maine / California, etc)__. *First we'll stop at Illinois. Then we'll stop at* __(Texas / Maine / California, etc)__.

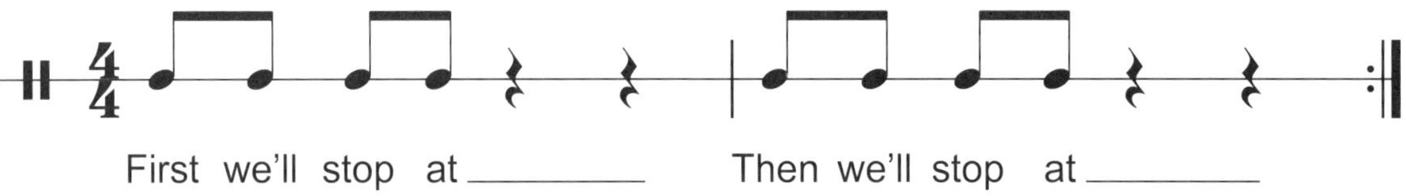

- *This time, you may choose both places you want the train to stop! Remember to say your full answer twice.*

- Students speak the rhyme while stepping a steady beat in a circle. At the B section, students stand still and speak their choices for where the train will stop.
    - **Note:** Students will give divergent answers, and speak their destinations at the same time.

CLASS 2

Objective: Students improvise a B section using a beat and a beat subdivision in a large ensemble

Assessment:

The student improvises a B section using a beat and a beat subdivision in a large ensemble	
3	The student improvises a B section using a beat and a beat subdivision in a large ensemble
1	The student does not improvise a B section using a beat and a beat subdivision in a large ensemble, or does not improvise

Process:

- Review previous class: Students stand in a circle and walk with a steady beat while speaking the rhyme.
- Next, students walk with a steady beat while clapping the rhythm of the words and inner hearing the rhyme.
- Motion for students to sit. *Let's improvise our own music using some places the train might stop.* Display state names on the board: Indiana, Illinois / Texas, Oklahoma / Georgia, Tennessee / Arizona, Utah

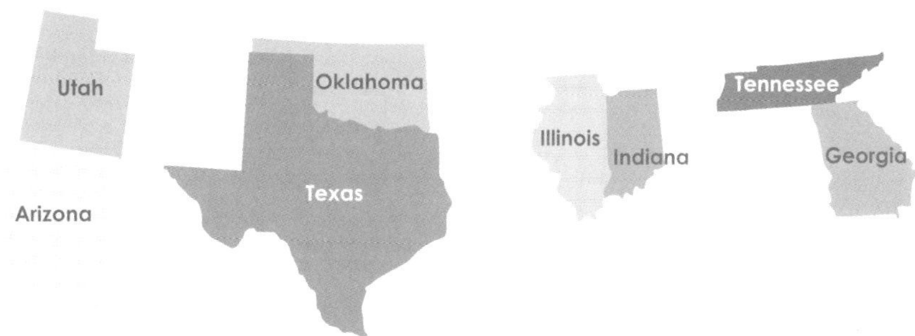

- The teacher improvises eight beats using two state choices and students echo while patting a steady beat.
  - **Examples:**

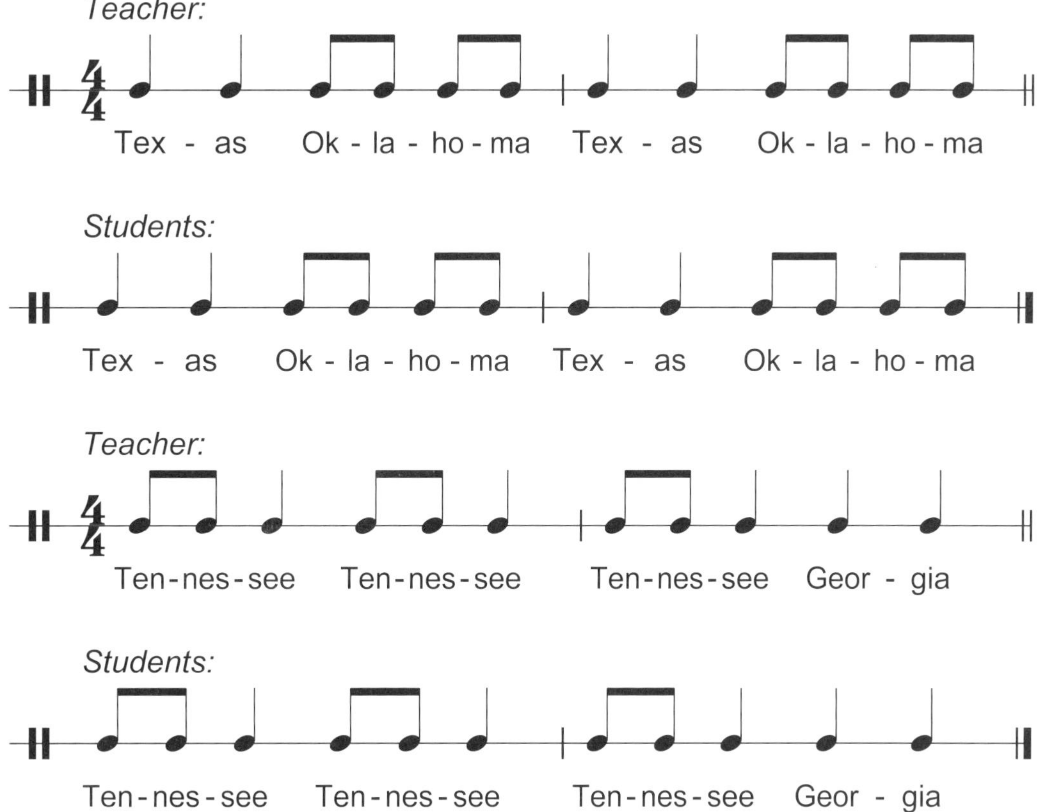

  - **Echoing Text Patterns:** If you observe students struggling to echo eight-beat patterns, consider using four-beat patterns instead. Also check to make sure all students are patting a steady beat as they listen and echo.
- After a few rounds, invite students to choose if they will echo the same rhythm, or improvise the words in a different order. Ask students to show their choice for their same or different response by holding up two hands. Hands together means they'll echo the same rhythm and hands apart means they'll improvise a different order.

- Speak the pattern again and listen to students echoing or improvising.
  - **Example improvisation:**

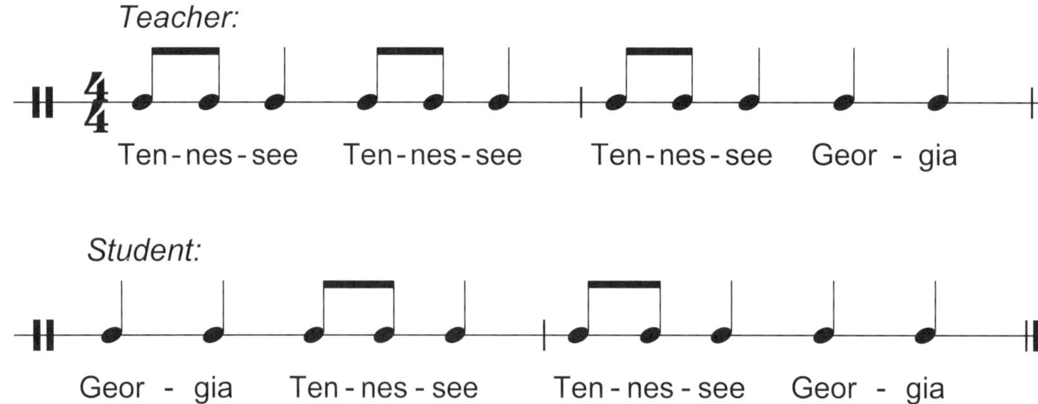

- Eventually, ask all students to improvise.
  - **SEL Self-Awareness:** *Does it feel easy or challenging for you to come up with a different response? Do you prefer to echo or to improvise?*
- Combine with the rhyme: Students scatter in open space. Student musicians walk in a steady beat around the classroom speaking the rhyme, creating their own train pathway in open space. When the rhyme is over, students stop in place. The teacher improvises an order of states on the board and students improvise a change.
  - **Locomotor Movement in Open Space:** Encourage musicians to move their trains around in open space. Open spaces are safe areas of the music room with plenty of empty air (not too near music friends, instruments, or other objects). If students show they are not yet ready to move in open space independently, consider asking one student leader to move the class around the room in a line.
- Continue several rounds of moving while speaking the rhyme, then stopping to improvise.

CLASS 3

Objective: Students improvise a beat and a beat subdivision with a partner

The student improvises a beat and a beat subdivision with a partner	
3	The student improvises a beat and a beat subdivision with a partner
1	The student does not improvise a beat and a beat subdivision with a partner, or does not improvise

Process:

- Review previous class: Students scatter in open space. Student musicians walk in a steady beat around the classroom speaking the rhyme. When the rhyme is over, students stop in place and improvise a response to the teacher's state name combination.
- Divide the class into two groups: *ones* and *twos*. Ask students to show their number on their fingers.
- As students speak the rhyme, they step a steady beat and walk to a music friend who does not have their number (*ones* find a partner who is a *two*. *Twos* find a partner who is a *one*).
- When the rhyme is over, the *one* student improvises an order of states on the board. The *two* student improvises a different response.

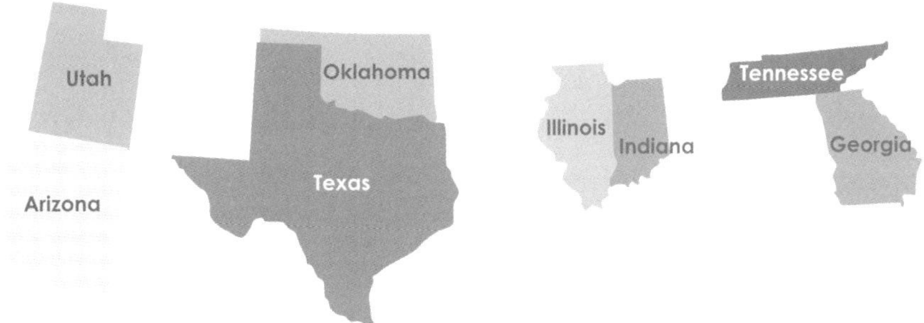

- Continue a few rounds, then ask students to switch numbers (*ones* become *twos*, *twos* become *ones*).
- Repeat stepping to find a partner while speaking the rhyme. The new *ones* improvise first and the new *twos* improvise second.
  - **Flexible Levels of Notational Literacy:** This improvisation uses a beat and a beat subdivision. If students can aurally identify the number of sounds on each beat of their improvisation, we can connect those sounds to rhythmic vocabulary of quarter notes and eighth notes.

Extension:

- Student improvisations can also be transferred to unpitched percussion such as hand drums or rhythm sticks.

Barred Instrument Improvisation with Do, Mi, Sol, La: Ickle Ockle

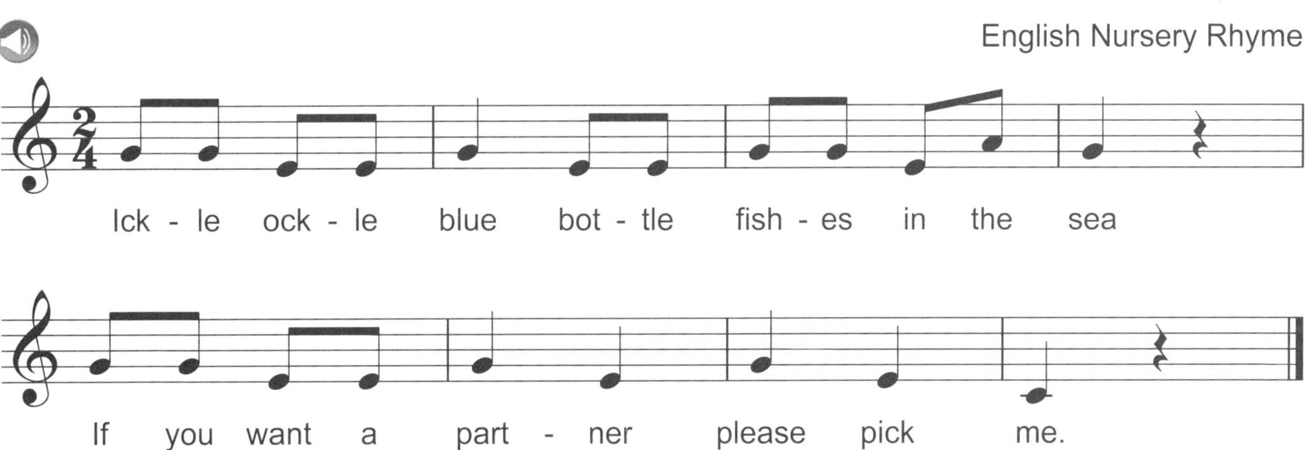

Game (by Victoria Boler): Students walk in open space singing the song. At the end of the song, each student joins hands with a partner. In the next round of the song, partners join with another group. Continue singing and combining groups until the class is in a circle.

Improvisation Project: Improvise with *do, mi, sol, la*

Preparing the Project:

- Before the project, students should have conscious knowledge of *mi, sol, la*, and have experience with *do*. Students should also be able to sing the song and play the game to Ickle Ockle without teacher assistance.
- **Teaching the Song:** Sing the song while students listen and pat a steady beat. Ask students to clap on the last word of the song ("me"). Ask students to sing the last four beats of the song ("please pick me") as you sing the rest. When students sing the last four beats tunefully, add the game. After several rounds of the game (perhaps in another class) transition to students singing the whole song without teacher assistance.

CLASS 1

Objective: Students aurally decode the melody of "Ickle Ockle"

Assessment:

The student aurally decodes the melody of "Ickle Ockle"	
4	The student aurally decodes the melody of "Ickle Ockle" with complete accuracy
3	The student aurally decodes the melody of "Ickle Ockle" with accuracy throughout most of the performance
2	The student aurally decodes the melody of "Ickle Ockle" with inaccuracies
1	The student does not play the melody in E minor pentatonic, or does not play

Process:

- Lead students in singing the song and playing the game
- When the game is over, ask students to move around the room with their partner in open space like fish swimming in the sea. Encourage students to think about how their fish might move in the water. Improvise a new melody to the rhythm of "Ickle Ockle" using *do, mi, sol,* and *la* on a metallophone, recorder, or a neutral syllable as students move.
  - **Open and Closed Space:** When students move, they should continuously look for open space, or space in the classroom that is empty. In contrast, closed space is already taken up by an object such as another music friend or an instrument.
- After a few moments, ask pairs of students to partner with another pair of students, creating a "school" of four fish.
- Display the fish color graphic and ask students to each choose a different color. Call one fish color to be the school leader. The lead fish moves their group around the room. Continue to improvise a new melody to the rhythm of "Ickle Ockle" using *do, mi, sol,* and *la* as students move.
  - **SEL Relationship Skills:** Musicians can sometimes have conflict when they make decisions. What will you do if two people in your group want to be the same color?

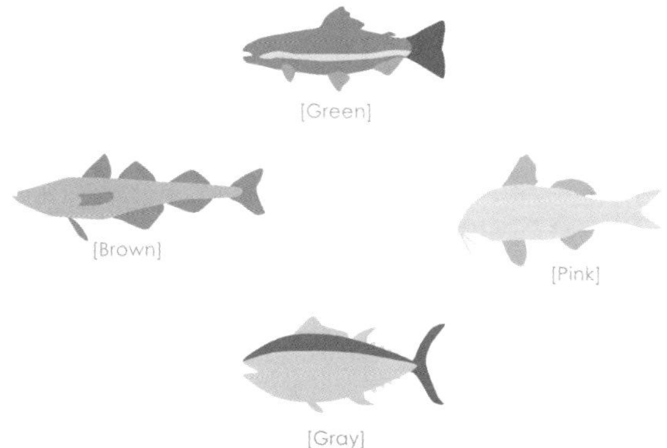

- Switch out the lead fish by calling different fish colors as time allows.
- After a few rounds, ask the group leader to move their school around to the melodic contour of the song, swimming up high for the high pitches and swimming down low for the lower pitches. All students sing the song on "loo" as they move.
- *What is the last word in our song?* ("Me.") *What can you tell me about this pitch?* (Answers will be divergent - it's the lowest pitch in our song.) *In this class, what do we call this low, home note?* (Do.)
  - **Flexible Levels of Notational Literacy:** If *do* is not conscious knowledge for students, consider asking them to sing the song and trace the melodic contour. Ask students to touch the floor on the lowest pitch in the song. Label this as *do* and show the hand sign.

- Seated, students work with their shoulder partner to sing the rest of the melody on solfege with hand signs. Give students a few moments to work, then ask students to check their answers by singing together as a class.
    - If students struggle to articulate the solfege syllables, take this in as useful assessment information! Sing the melody four beats at a time on a neutral syllable like "loo." Sing students' starting solfege syllable and show its hand sign.

    - **SEL Self-Management:** *Do you notice that it is easy or challenging for you to hear the song and sing it on solfege syllables? If it feels too challenging, what are some things I can do as your teacher to help you? If it feels too easy, what are some things I can do as your teacher to make it more interesting?*
- With a barred instrument visual, review steps and skips and identify the placement of *do*, *mi*, *sol*, and *la* if *do* is on C.

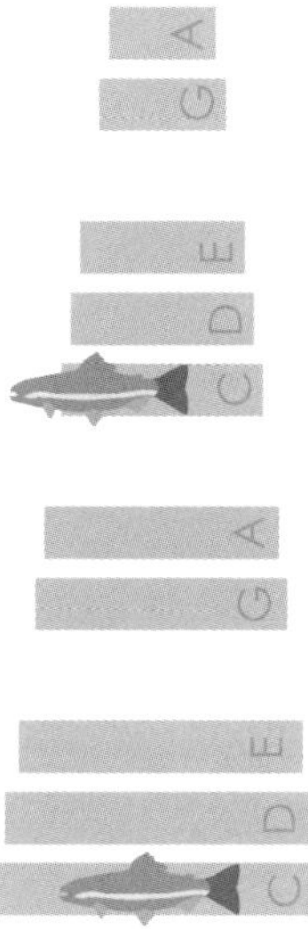

- Sing the song while pointing to the barred instrument.

CLASS 2

Objective: Students improvise a melodic contour using *do*, *mi*, *sol*, and *la* in an ensemble setting

Assessment:

The student improvises a melodic contour using *do*, *mi*, *sol*, and *la* in an ensemble setting	
3	The student improvises a melodic contour using *do*, *mi*, *sol*, and *la* in an ensemble setting
1	The student does not improvise a melodic contour using *do*, *mi*, *sol*, and *la* in an ensemble setting, or does not improvise

Materials: Barred instruments set up in C pentatonic (enough for students to share with a partner)

Process:

- Lead students in singing the song and playing the game.
- Seated with their partner, students review singing the song on solfege syllables with hand signs. Sing the song on solfege as a class.

- With students seated, display one of the melodic contour exploration graphics. Ask students to think about what the melody would sound like, then vocalize their idea.

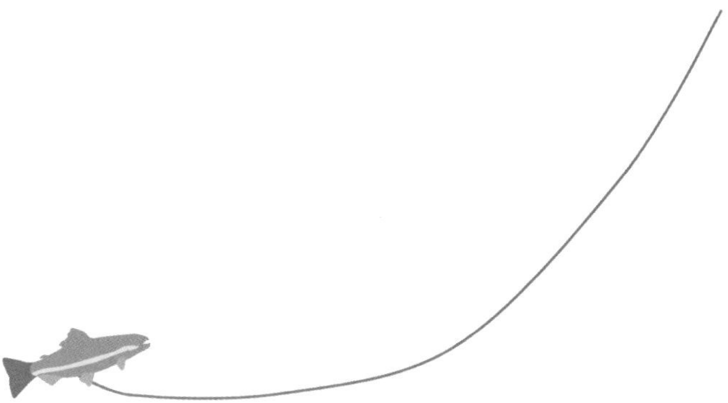

- Repeat with several graphics of different melodic contour options.

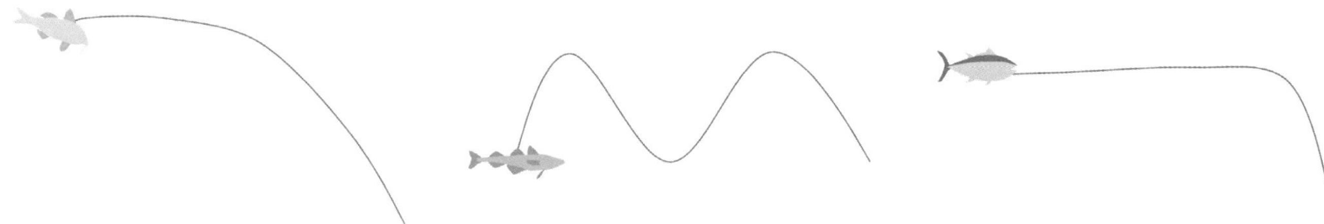

- Display the graphic with all the melodic contour options. With their partner, students choose their two favorite melodic contour shapes.

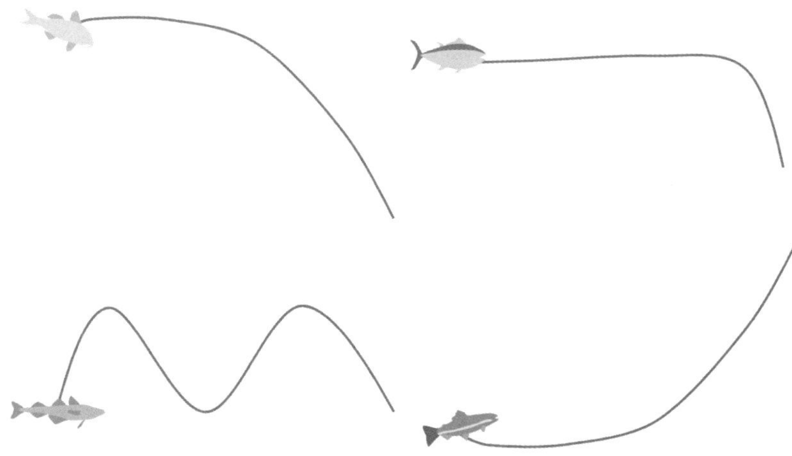

- Motion for students to stand and ask them to move around the room in open space with their partner as they show the first shape of their favorite melodic contour through movement and vocalization. Ask students to freeze after their first shape. Give a signal (like finger cymbals or a chime) to continue moving and vocalizing their second shape.
- Ask students to sing the song as they move to a barred instrument with their partner.

  SEL Self-Management: Students may still be working on the self-management of walking to barred instruments independently. If this is the case, walk around the room as students perform their vocal exploration movements with their partner. Tap pairs of students on the shoulder as a signal to move. Continue until all students are seated behind an instrument.

- Seated behind instruments set up in C pentatonic, give students a few moments to explore and to find the pitches from the song: *do, mi, sol,* and *la* with *do* on C. Students work with their partner to identify the correct bars, with both students sitting behind an instrument. Notice there are two sets of *do, mi, sol,* and *la*. Students may choose which set they'll use.

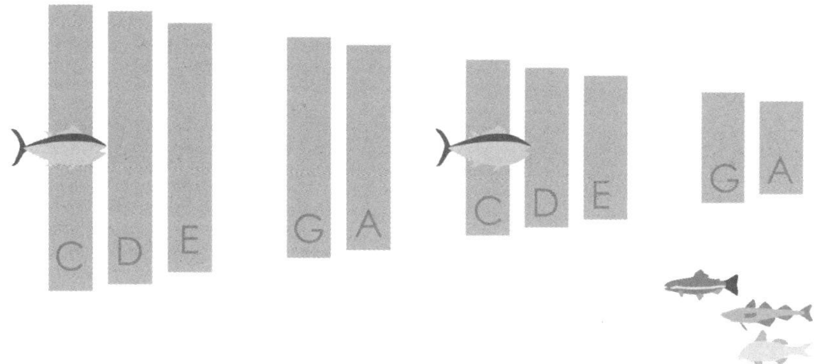

- Students place the mallets on the ground behind them. Lead students in checking their answers by improvising eight beats after a rhythmic prompt. Both students tap the bars in response.

  - Continue through *sol* and *la*.
- Lead students in playing the rhythm of the song on *do*.

- Next, ask one partner to play the first phrase on *do* and the other to play the second phrase on *do*.
  - If students aren't yet aware of an eight-beat phrase, ask them to notice the steady beat of the song and figure out where they take a breath. Guide students to articulate that they take a breath on beats 8 and 16. The beats where we breathe mark the end of the two phrases for this song.

- Show the graphic of each melodic contour option.

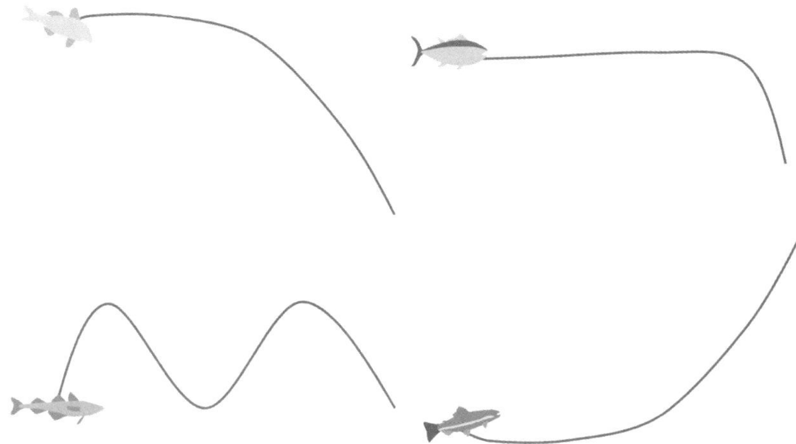

- Ask each student to choose their favorite melody shape and experiment with playing it on their instrument. One partner plays the first phrase and the other partner plays the second phrase with the melodic contour of their choice.
- Invite a few students to pick up mallets and share their melody improvisations with the rest of the class.
  - **SEL Social Awareness:** *If you were sharing your improvisation with the class, how would you want the class to respond? How can we make music class a place where musicians are excited to improvise?*
- Ask students to take the mallets from behind them. Lead the whole class in improvising a new melody to the rhythm of the song, based on the melodic contour they choose. One student plays the first phrase, the other plays the second phrase.

CLASS 3

Objective: Students improvise using *do, mi, sol,* and *la* in a rondo

Assessment:

The student improvises a melodic contour using *do, mi, sol,* and *la* in an ensemble setting	
3	The student improvises a melodic contour using *do, mi, sol,* and *la* in an ensemble setting
1	The student does not improvise a melodic contour using *do, mi, sol,* and *la* in an ensemble setting, or does not improvise

Materials: Barred instruments set up in C pentatonic (enough for students to share with a partner)

Process:

- Create a "fish bowl" by placing barred instruments in a circle around the room.

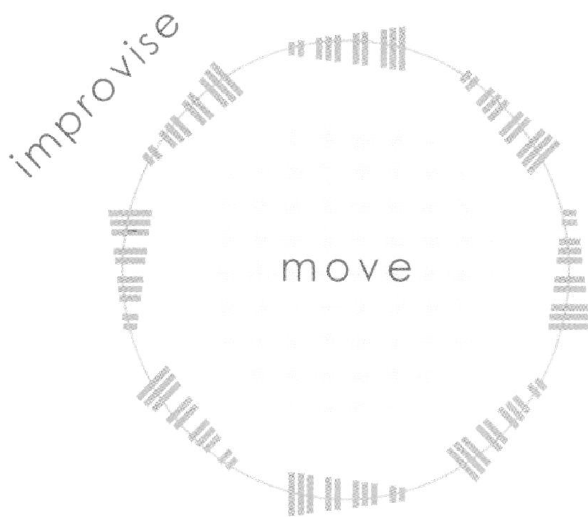

- Display the melodic contour options on the board.

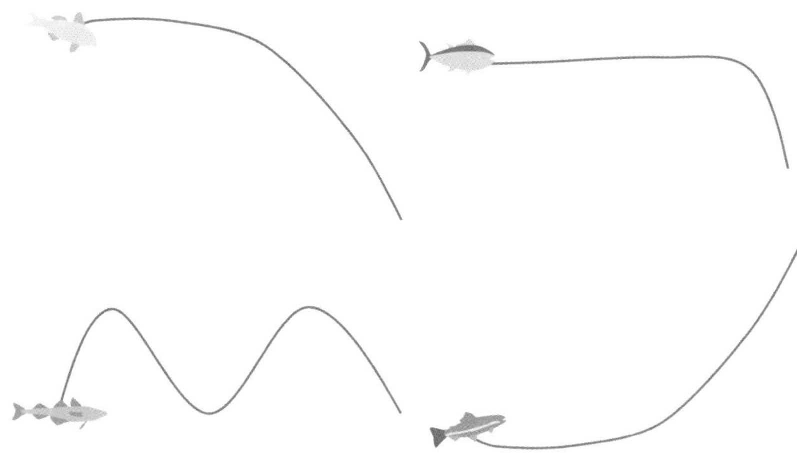

- Seated with a partner behind an instrument, students take turns improvising melodies to both phrases of "Ickle Ockle" using their favorite two melodic contour shapes on the board.
- With their partner, decide who will move first. That student walks into the middle of the "fish bowl."
- Improvise in ABAB: All students sing the song as the A section. During the B section, the students at the barred instruments improvise their melody idea while their partner swims around in the fish bowl. During the next A section, partners switch jobs.
    - If space is limited in your teaching situation, the students in the middle may sit down or stand in place and show their movements in a non-locomotor way.

IMPROVISATION: UPPER ELEMENTARY

Body Percussion Improvisation with Ta-dimi: Draw a Bucket of Water

English Singing Game

Additional Verses:

Number one goes under... Number two goes under... Number three goes under...
Number four goes under.....

Game: Students stand in groups of four. Players 1 and 2 face each other, players 3 and 4 face each other. Players 1 and 2 take hands. Players 3 and 4 take hands above the hands of players 1 and 2. All students sing the song. At "number one goes under," player 1 walks under the hands of players 3 and 4. At "number two goes under," player two walks under the hands of players 3 and 4. At "number three goes under," player 3 walks under the hands of players 1 and 2. At "number four goes under," player four walks under the hands of players 1 and 2.

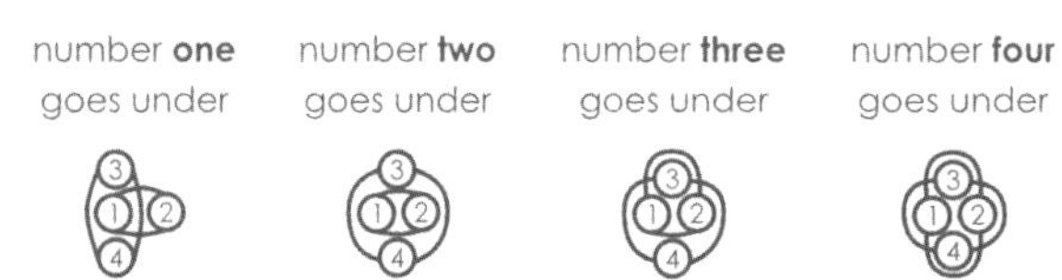

Improvisation Project: Improvise with *ta-dimi*

Preparing the Project:

- Before the project, students should have conscious knowledge of steady beat, rhythm, rhythm vs beat, quarter notes, beamed eighth notes, and an eighth note followed by two sixteenth notes. They should also be able to sing and play the game to "Draw a Bucket of Water" without teacher assistance.
- **Teaching the Game:** In their groups, lead students in singing the song without taking hands. At "number one goes under," player 1 steps into the middle of the group. Continue through the verses. When students are ready, ask them to join hands and play the full game.

CLASS 1

Objective: Students aurally identify *ta-dimi* in unknown rhythmic material

Assessment:

The student aurally identifies *ta-dimi* in new rhythmic material	
3	The student aurally identifies *ta-dimi* in new rhythmic material
1	The student incorrectly identifies *ta-dimi* in new material or does not verbalize rhythm syllables

Process:

- Lead students in singing the song and playing the game.
- After the game, pat and clap improvised four-beat rhythms using *ta-dimi*. The class echoes the rhythm on body percussion of their choice.
  - **Rhythm examples:**

  - **Student Choice as a Step Toward Improvisation:** Students may use their own combination of snapping, clapping, patting, and stamping to echo the pattern.
- After a few rounds of echoing, ask students to choose if they'll (1) continue to echo the rhythm on body percussion of their choice, or (2) change the rhythm. Ask students to show their choice on their fingers by holding up a one or a two.
- Continue improvising four-beat rhythms that use *ta-dimi* and listen to the class response.
  - Pay attention to students who choose to improvise, and listen to whether or not they include *ta-dimi* organically in their improvisations. Note that students do not necessarily need to know that they are using *ta-dimi* in order to use it spontaneously.
- Consider asking a student volunteer to lead the patterns.
- After a few rounds of echoing, perform a four-beat rhythm using *ta-dimi*. Ask the class to think the rhythm in their heads, and then speak it out loud on rhythm syllables. This will create four beats of silence before students' response.

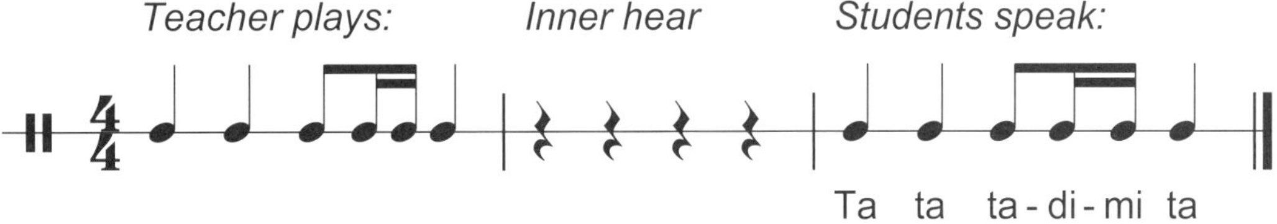

  - **SEL Self-Awareness:** *Is it easy or challenging to echo the rhythms on rhythmic syllables? If it's challenging, what supports would help you?* (Working with a friend, patting a steady beat, using a slower tempo.)
- Listen to students aurally identify ta-dimi in the unknown rhythmic material.
  - **Flexible Levels of Notational Literacy:** If *ta-dimi* is not conscious knowledge for students, invite students to notice the "long short short" pattern in"one in a bush and two in a bush." Label this long short short pattern as *ta-dimi* and speak the last phrase on rhythm syllables.

CLASS 2

Objective: Students perform four-beat rhythms using *ta-dimi*.

Assessment:

The student performs *ta-dimi* in a four-beat rhythm.	
4	The student performs *ta-dimi* in a four-beat rhythm with accurate articulation
3	The student performs *ta-dimi* in a four-beat rhythm; some articulations of the rhythm may be slightly out of time
2	The student performs *ta-dimi* in a four-beat rhythm with approximate articulation
1	The student does not perform

Process:

- Ask students to sing the song while getting into groups of four.
- Seated in their groups, students sing the song and pat the rhythm of the words.
- After singing the song, sight-read the rhythms on the board using rhythm syllables and body percussion of students' choice. Count students off with a *ta-dimi* rhythm, such as:

Creating a Rhythmic Context: Notice that the first rhythm matches "one in a bush and two in a bush and." Notice that the last rhythm matches the count off, "one and a two and a here you play." These will likely be the easiest rhythms for students to read.

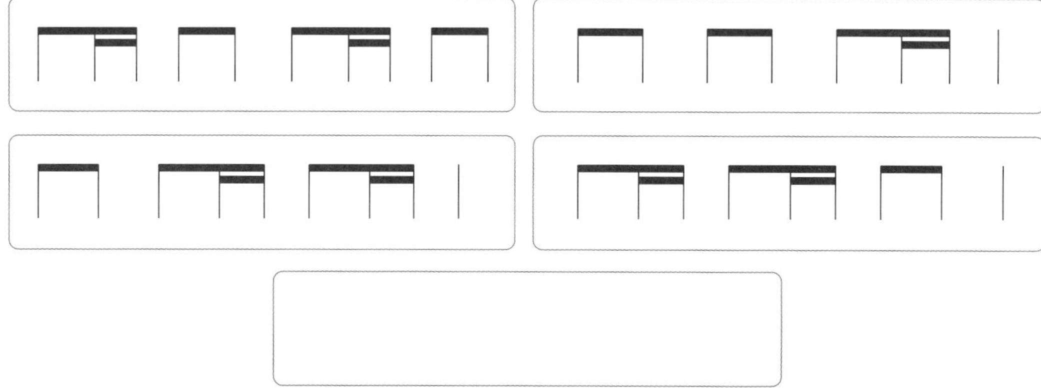

- *What do these rhythms have in common?* (Answers may be divergent. Point out that all rhythms use *ta-dimi*.)
- Next, ask students to choose two of their favorite rhythms to play, or play an improvisation. Count students off with and listen to the class perform their eight beats.

- In their groups, ask students to come up with their own four-beat rhythm idea that uses *ta-dimi*.
- When students are ready, ask one member of each group to come to the board and write their group's rhythm. Ask the students seated in their groups to give a thumbs up if the notation matches the rhythm they came up with, and a sideways thumb if there are changes that need to be made.
- When the rhythms are notated on the board, practice reading each rhythm together as a class using rhythm syllables and body percussion of students' choice.

- In their groups, ask students to number off from one to four as if they're going to play the game, and hold up fingers to show their number.

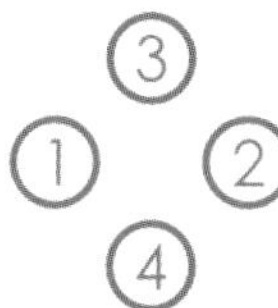

- When students have their numbers assigned, sing the song again.
- At the end of the song, the student musician who is "number one" chooses a pattern from the board to read, or chooses to improvise their own pattern using *ta-dimi*. The other students in the group take turns echoing, passing the rhythm around. (Number one reads the pattern, number two copies the pattern, number three copies the pattern, then number four copies the pattern.)
- Repeat the song four times so each student in the group has a chance to solo a pattern on the board, or improvise their own pattern. During the activity, walk around the room and listen to students perform *ta-dimi* in a four-beat rhythm.

  Scaffolding Improvisation: In this class segment, students have had multiple opportunities to improvise if they choose. All students engage with the target rhythm, *ta-dimi*, but right now they may choose their level of musical choice through body percussion, choosing their rhythm, or improvising.

CLASS 3

Objective: Students use *ta-dimi* in a four-beat rhythmic improvisation

Assessment:

The student uses *ta-dimi* in a four-beat rhythmic improvisation	
3	The student uses *ta-dimi* in a four-beat rhythmic improvisation
1	The student does not use *ta-dimi* in a four-beat rhythmic improvisation, or does not play

Materials: Tubanos or other standing hand drum (one per group)

Process:

- Seated in their groups, students sing the song.
- After singing the song, all students do a practice round of improvising four beats on body percussion. (All students improvise at the same time.)
- Repeat the practice improvisation and ask students to use *ta-dimi* in their improvisation.
- In their groups, ask students to number off from one to four as if they're going to play the game, and hold up fingers to show their number.
- When students have their numbers assigned, choose one number to get a tubano (or other hand drum) and bring it back to the group.

  This activity uses one tubano or other hand drum per student group. If more instruments are available in your situation, each student may have a hand drum. If necessary, take a few moments to review hand drum technique. As students play, they should bounce their hands off the drum, but keep the bounces small and close to the drum head so they can play articulately.

- Sing the first verse of the song. At "number one goes under," the student musician who is number one improvises four beats, including *ta-dimi*. The rest of the students in the group take turns echoing number one's improvisation.
- Continue singing the other verses of the song, giving each student a chance to improvise with *ta-dimi* when their number is called; i.e. - number two goes under: number two improvises and the rest of the group takes turns echoing.

- **SEL Social Awareness:** *How do you think the people in your group might feel before they improvise as a solo? What can we do to support them before, during, and after their improvisation?*

- *Did you include* ta-dimi *in your improvisation?* Students show a thumbs up if they did, a thumbs down if they did not, and a sideways thumb if they're not sure.

Extension:

- For an extra challenge, repeat the activity. This time, every person in the group makes a change to the rhythm instead of echoing.

Barred Instrument Improvisation with Ta-di--di: Alabama Gal

Additional Verses:

I don't know how how (x3).... Alabama gal
I'll show you how how (x3)..... Alabama gal
Ain't I rock candy (x3) .... Alabama gal

Play Party Directions:

- **Formation:** Students stand in two lines facing a partner. The pair at the front of the line is the "head pair." The end of the line is the "foot."
- Verse 1: The head pair joins hands and moves toward the foot for eight beats, then all the way back up to their original places for eight beats. The rest of the class sings and claps a steady beat.
- Verse 2: All partners right arm swing for eight beats, then left arm swing for eight beats while singing.
- Verse 3: All students face the front of the line. The head of each line turns outward and leads their line toward the foot, with all students following and singing the song.
- Verse 4: When the head pair gets to the foot, they join hands to create an arch. The lines of students following go through the arch while singing the song. This creates a new head pair and the play party begins again.

Improvisation Project: Improvise with *ta-di--di*

Preparing the Project:

- Before the project, students should have conscious knowledge of steady beat, rhythm, rhythm vs beat, quarter notes, beamed eighth notes, quarter rests, and have experience with syncopation (eight, quarter, eighth, or *ta-di--di*). Students should also be able to sing the song and perform the play party to "Alabama Gal" without teacher assistance.
- **Introducing the Play Party:** Teach the play party with all students standing in a single circle, facing in. Sing the melody on a neutral syllable as students listen and move with simultaneous imitation. Verse 1: All students walk in for eight beats, then out for eight beats. Verse 2: Students turn in a stationary circle to the right for eight beats, then left for eight beats. Verse 3 and 4: Students all turn to the right and walk in a circle through the end of the song.

CLASS 1

Objective: Students improvise a change to an eight-beat rhythmic prompt

Assessment:

The student improvises a change to the eight-beat rhythmic prompt	
3	The student improvises a change to the eight-beat rhythmic prompt
1	The student does not improvise a change to the eight-beat rhythmic prompt, or does not participate

Process:

- Lead students in singing the song and performing the play party.
- At the end of each round of the game, improvise an eight-beat body percussion rhythm using *ta-di--di*. Ask students to improvise a change to the rhythm as a response, such as keeping the rhythm the same and changing the body percussion, or improvising a new rhythm.
  - **Example Changes:**

  - **SEL Self-Awareness:** Musicians can encounter rhythmic challenges! Student musicians here may choose the appropriate level of challenge for their current rhythmic skillset and musical interest. Students may choose to echo the teacher's rhythm but change the body percussion combinations. Students may also choose to create an entirely new rhythmic response. For the purposes of this activity, both improvisations are acceptable.
- After a few rounds, ask students to listen for whether or not the improvisation prompt uses *ta-di--di*. (It does.)
  - **Flexible Levels of Notational Literacy:** If *ta-di--di* is an unknown rhythmic pattern for students, listen to them use it accurately as they sing the song and perform the play party to Alabama Gal. Notice whether or not they accurately echo *ta-di--di* in the body percussion patterns at the end of the song, or if they incorporate it into their own rhythmic improvisation. Draw students' attention to the "short-long-short long long" rhythm throughout the song, such as "I don't know how how." Label this rhythmic pattern as *ta-di--di*.
- Seated, ask students to pat a steady beat and inner hear the first verse of the song. As they inner hear, challenge students to listen for how many times in the rhythm, *ta-di--di* is used. (The correct answer is three times.)

- Seated, ask students to check their answer by singing the song on rhythm syllables instead of text.
  - *(ta-di - di ta ta, ta-di - di ta ta, ta-di - di ta ta, ta-di ta-di ta rest)*
- Sing the song and play the game. This time, one line of students improvises an eight-beat rhythm on body percussion and their partner in the other line improvises an eight-beat response.
- After the first round, ask students to think about whether or not they used *ta-di--di* in their improvisation.
  - **Note:** Students may choose to use the target rhythm in their improvisation, or leave it out. The purpose of this improvisation is aural awareness.
- Repeat the improvisation activity with each round of the game as time allows.

CLASS 2

Objective: Students improvise on barred instruments using *ta-di--di* in an ensemble

Assessment:

Students improvise on barred instruments using *ta-di--di*	
3	The student improvises on a barred instrument using *ta-di--di*
1	The student does not improvise on a barred instrument using *ta-di--di*, or does not improvise

Materials: Barred instruments set up in F pentatonic (enough for each student, or pairs of students)

Process:

- Lead students in singing the song and performing the play party.
- After each round of the game, one line of students improvises an eight-beat rhythm on body percussion and the other line of students improvises an eight-beat response.
- Ask students to improvise a rhythm on body percussion as they move to stand behind a barred instrument set up in F pentatonic.

  - **Working with Limited Instruments:** Two students may sit behind a barred instrument and take turns if instruments are limited. Students waiting for their turn may play body percussion instead of barred instruments.
- Give students a few moments to experiment playing the barred instruments in F pentatonic. As students play, walk around the room and check the setup of the barred instruments.
- After a few moments, lead students in playing a chord bordun as they sing the first verse of the song. (Students should be able to hear the song above the chord bordun.)

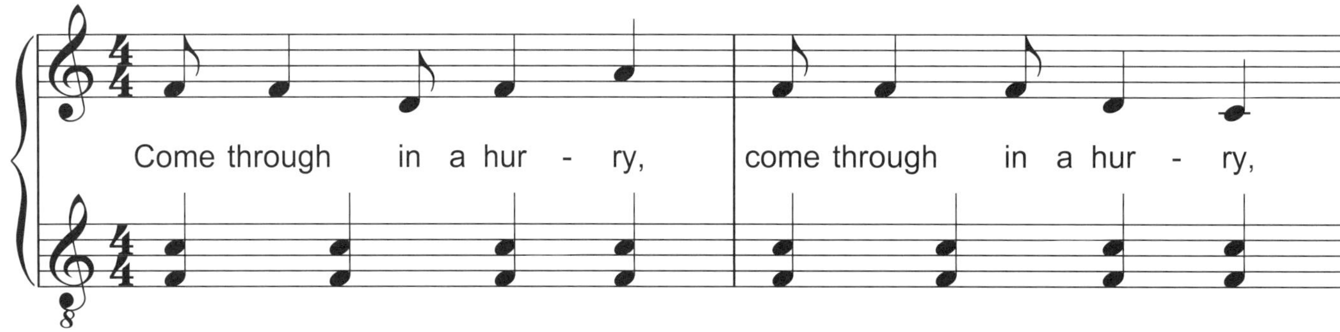

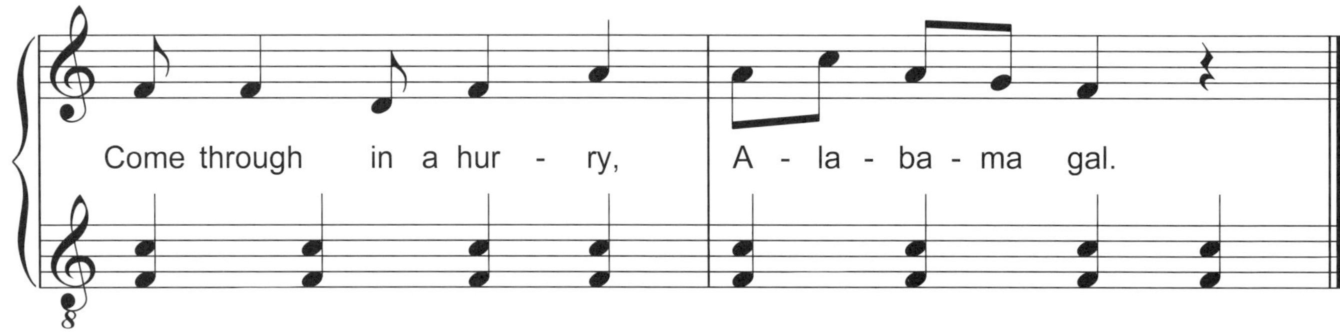

- **Note:** if students are not aware of what a chord bordun is, you can ask them to keep a steady beat on F and the C above it. If students have conscious knowledge of borduns, the class might choose another option instead, like a broken bordun, level bordun, or arpeggiated bordun.

- After the first verse, improvise an eight-beat rhythm on F, using *ta-di--di*. Students improvise their own eight-beat rhythmic response on F.

  - **Improvisation and Critical Thinking:** *How similar to the first rhythm can you make your improvisation, while still making a change? How different can you make your rhythm? The song says to come through in a hurry. What would your rhythm sound like if it were in a hurry? What would it sound like if it weren't in a hurry?*

- Next, invite students to use any pitches they want in their improvisation response. Sing the first verse while playing the chord bordun. After the first verse, improvise eight beats using more pitches in the pentatone and incorporating *ta-di--di*. Listen as students improvise their own response.
- Ask students to notice whether or not they include the target rhythm, *ta-di--di* in their improvisations for the rest of the class.
- Divide the class in half.
- Lead students in playing a chord bordun softly as they sing the first verse of the song. Then, one half of the class improvises an eight-beat melody. The other half improvises an eight-beat response.
- Repeat the activity. This time after singing the first verse and playing the bordun, the first half of the class plays their improvisations ending on *sol* (C). The second half of the class plays their improvisations, ending on *do* (F).
- Switch jobs.
- Invite students to have their own conversations with themselves! After singing the first verse of the song and quietly playing a chord bordun, students improvise sixteen beats on the barred instrument. The first eight beats end on *sol* (C) and the next eight beats end on *do* (F).
- Ask students to show a thumbs up if they improvised with *ta-di--di*, a thumbs down if they did not, and a sideways thumb if they're not sure.

  - **SEL Self-Awareness:** We can help students scaffold their improvisation responses by giving musical options. In this mallet improvisation progression, students move from body percussion to improvising on barred instruments in question and answer form. Students may choose their appropriate level of challenge by creating rhythmically simple or rhythmically complex rhythms, and by expanding or limiting the number of pitches they use.

CLASS 3

Objective: Students improvise solos using *ta-di--di.*

Assessment:

The student improvises a solo using *ta-di--di*	
3	The student improvises a solo using *ta-di--di*
1	The student does not improvise a solo using *ta-di--di*

Materials: Barred instruments set up in F pentatonic (one for each grouop of four)

Process:

- Ask students to sing the song as they move to sit behind barred instruments set up in F pentatonic.
- Give students a few moments to play independently on their instruments as they review the previous class. As students explore, walk around the room and give feedback on the improvisations you hear.
  - **SEL Social Awareness:** Tell students that in this lesson segment they'll improvise solos that use *ta-di--di* in rondo form. What might a classmate feel right before they improvise? What might they feel right after they improvise? *What can we do to support each other?* (Give a smile after someone improvises, sing the song to set the musical context, pat a steady beat while the improviser plays, etc.)
- Review the previous class: Sing the first verse of the song while quietly playing a chord bordun. Then, students improvise sixteen beats, ending the first eight beats on *sol* (C) and the next eight beats on *do* (F). Ask students to include *ta-di--di* in their improvisation.
- Ask students to get into a group of four. Ask students to take one barred instrument for their group and move to an open spot in the room.
- In their group, students sit in a circle around the barred instrument.
- *How will we know we've done a good job with our performance?* Work together as a class to create a small checklist (three to five items) of criteria. Write students' assessment criteria on the board.
  - Sample criteria might be:
    We use *ta-di--di* somewhere in the improvisation
    We play with a steady beat
    We play two eight-beat phrases
- Perform improvisations in a rondo. Students sing the song and pat a steady beat. In between each verse, one student in the group improvises 16 beats on the barred instrument, incorporating *ta-di--di.* During the verses, students rotate who is seated behind the barred instrument. Consider playing a chord bordun or a hand drum to keep time during the improvisations.
- After the activity, ask students to show a thumbs up if they improvised with *ta-di--di,* a thumbs down if they did not, and a sideways thumb if they're not sure.

Extensions:

- Consider videoing student improvisations to share with the school community after getting written administrative and guardian permission.
- Add the improvisations with the play party. Students sing the song and perform the play party. At the end of each full round, the pair at the foot of the line improvises sixteen beats, then rejoins the line to play the next round.

Recorder Improvisation in E Minor Pentatonic: Humpty Dumpty

English Nursery Rhyme

Improvisation Project: E minor recorder improvisation

Preparing the Project:

- Before the project, students should have conscious knowledge of *low la, do, re,* and *mi*. Students should have experience playing *low la, do, re,* and *mi* on recorder in la-based minor on E (the pitches are E, G, A, and B). Students should also be able to speak the rhyme to "Humpty Dumpty" without teacher assistance. The project is in 6/8 time, but students do not need to know the time signature in order to engage with the material.

CLASS 1

Objective: Improvise a melody in E minor pentatonic

Assessment:

The student improvises a melody to "Humpty Dumpty" in E minor pentatonic	
3	The student improvises a melody to "Humpty Dumpty" in E minor pentatonic
1	The student does not improvise a melody to "Humpty Dumpty" in E minor pentatonic, or does not improvise

Materials: Barred instruments set up in G pentatonic (enough for pairs of students to share), recorders

Process:

- Lead students in speaking the rhyme while clapping the rhythm of the words
- Ask students to partner with another classmate.
  - **SEL Social Awareness:** *When you think about who your partner will be for this activity, who do you hope to work with? What do you appreciate about that person? What makes someone a good musical partner? If you don't get to work with your very favorite person in the class, how can you be a good musical partner with whoever you do work with? What would it look like to appreciate that person just as much?*
- With a partner, students arrange a steady beat for body percussion of their choice.
  - **Examples:**

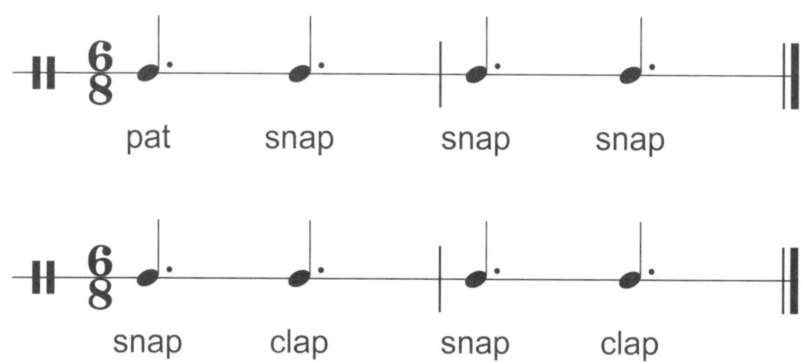

- Students speak the rhyme while performing the body percussion pattern with their partner.
- Ask students to move with their partner to barred instruments while performing their body percussion pattern. Both partners sit behind an instrument.
- In pairs at barred instruments, instruct student musicians to work together to set up in E-minor pentatonic, referencing the visual on the board if necessary.

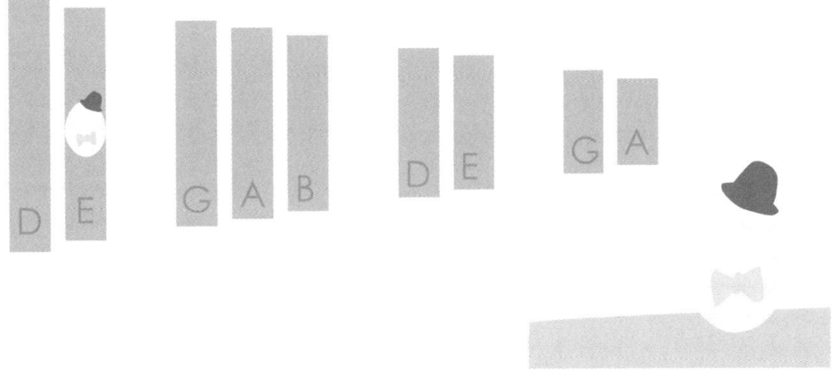

- When they're set up, invite students to take turns improvising around the instrument. As students explore free improvisation, walk around the room and check work as necessary.
  - **Creative Connections to Pedagogy:** This is a good time to review interval relationships on barred instruments. If E is *la*, then *do* is a skip above E on G. If G is *do*, then *re* is a step above G on A. If A is *re*, then *mi* is a step above A on B, and so on.
- Ask students to check their work by improvising on *low la*, *do*, *re*, and *mi*. Students begin with their low E:

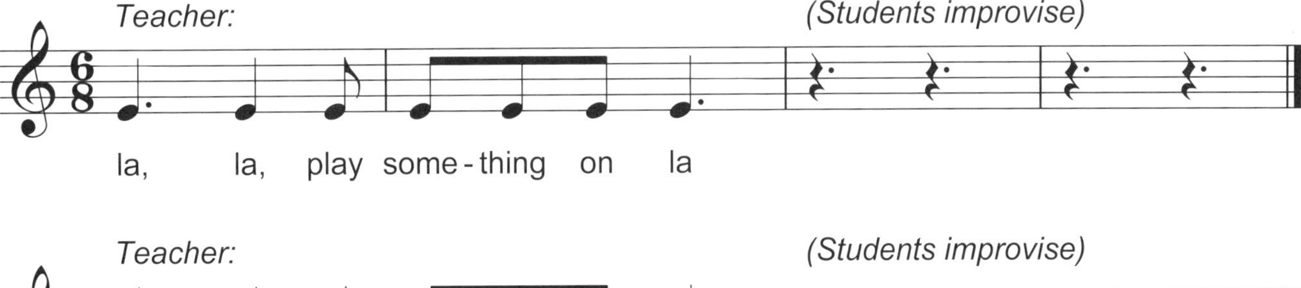

  - Continue with *re* and *mi*
- One student plays the rhythm of the rhyme on low E while the other partner performs the body percussion steady beat pattern. Switch jobs.
- Ask students to walk to a new barred instrument so they're working with a different partner.
- In their new pairs, one student musician improvises a melody to the rhythm of the words. The other student musician performs their steady beat pattern. Switch jobs.
  - **Improvisation Choices:** If necessary, review which note is the "home note" right now (*la*). *What happens if we end our improvisation on* la? (The piece will sound more final, like the improvisation is over.) *What will happen if we end on a pitch other than* la? (The piece may not sound as complete.) Students choose how they will end their improvisation, based on their musical goals.

CLASS 2

Objective: Students echo melodies in E minor pentatonic on recorder by ear

Assessment:

The student plays melodies in E minor pentatonic on recorder by ear	
4	The student plays melodies in E minor pentatonic on recorder by ear with complete accuracy
3	The student plays melodies in E minor pentatonic on recorder by ear with accuracy throughout most of the performance
2	The student plays melodies in E minor pentatonic on recorder by ear with inaccuracies
1	The student does not play the melody in E minor pentatonic, or does not play

Materials: Recorders

Process:

- Show the rhythmic building blocks on the board. Lead students in speaking each pattern.
  - **Flexible Levels of Notational Literacy:** There are multiple options for the notation of these rhythms. Since the purpose of the improvisation activity is improvisation in E minor pentatonic, you may choose the rhythmic representation that is the most suitable for your students.

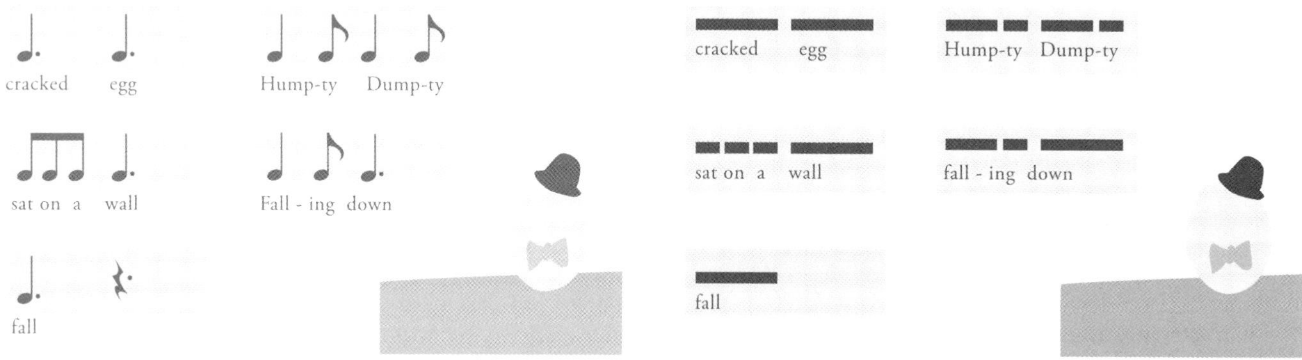

- As a class, students choose the order of two rhythmic building blocks. Lead students in speaking the order four times in a row. Students may choose their own body percussion combinations as they speak the rhythms.
  - **Example:**

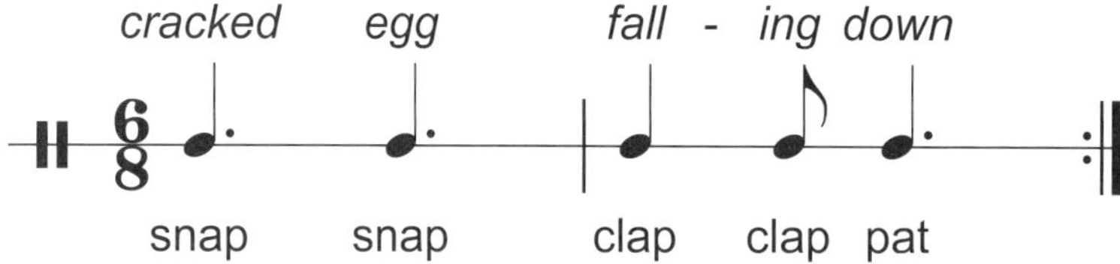

- With a partner, student musicians review low E, G, A, and B on their recorders, using the visual as a reference.

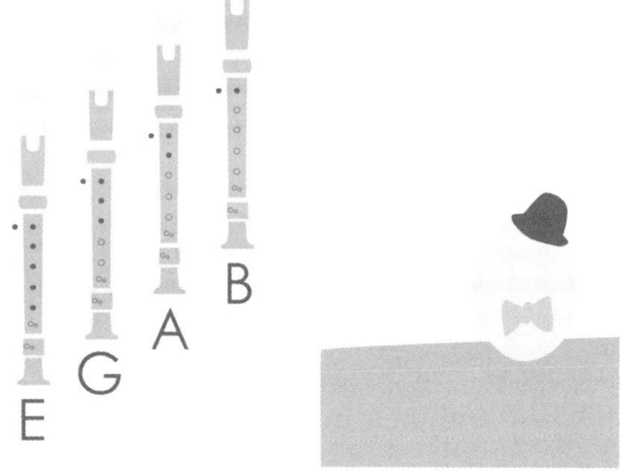

- Lead students in playing the student-arranged rhythm four times in a row on low E.
  - **Example:**

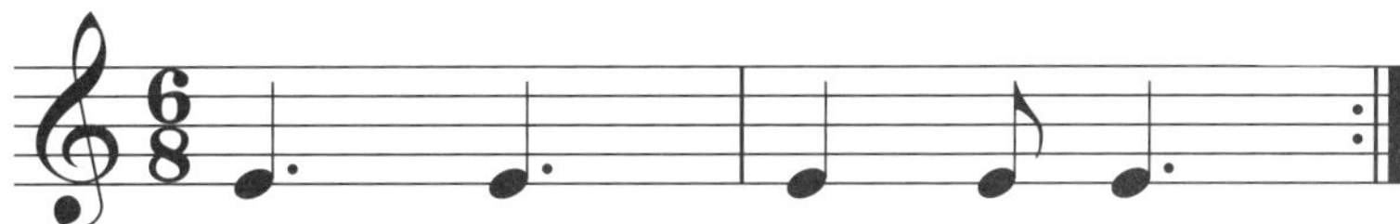

- Next, use the student-arranged rhythm and improvise in E-minor pentatonic. Students echo the patterns by ear.
  - **Scaffolding Recorder Performance and Aural Skills:** If you observe that students struggle to play the patterns by ear, narrow the pitches used to low E and G. For example:

  - Gradually add in more pitches as students are ready to aurally identify them and play them on their instrument.If necessary, it can also be helpful to sing the pattern on solfege and show the fingerings on the recorder without playing. Student musicians echo sing on a neutral syllable while showing the fingerings. After echo singing the pattern, try echo playing the same pattern on the recorder.
- With a partner or in a small group, ask students to come up with their own order of four rhythmic building blocks and perform them on E.

CLASS 3

Objective: Students improvise melodies on recorder in E minor pentatonic

Assessment:

The student improvises a melody on recorder in E minor pentatonic	
3	The student improvises a melody on recorder in E minor pentatonic
1	The student does not improvise a melody on recorder in E minor pentatonic

Materials: Rhythmic building blocks, recorders

Process:

- Show the rhythmic building blocks on the board.

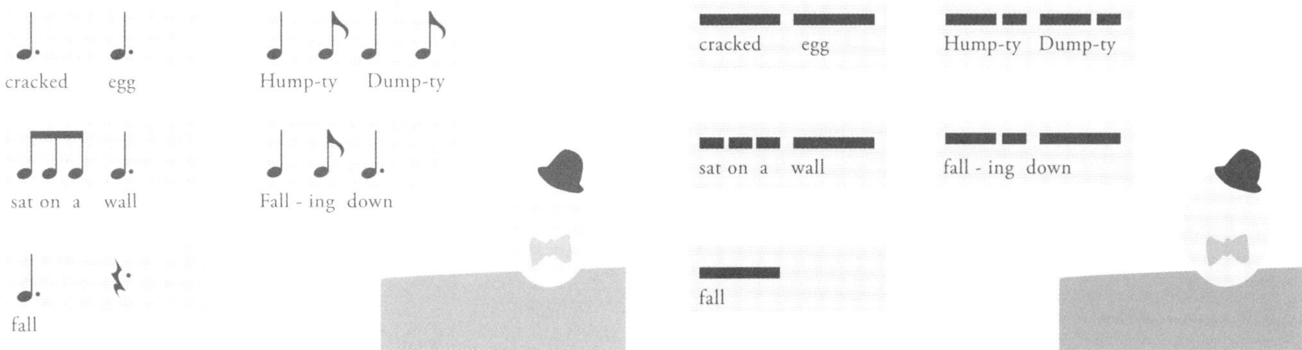

- As a class, decide on an arrangement of four building blocks. Practice performing the arrangement on recorders using low E.
  - **Recorder Performance:** Encourage students to use short articulations when performing the rhythm, so that the rhythm is crisp and clear the whole time.
- In a group of four, student musicians arrange four rhythmic building blocks.

- When everyone in the group can speak the rhythm, perform it on low E, two times in a row.
- Lead students in checking their rhythmic work by having all students perform their arrangements on low E at the same time, two times in a row. Listen for students starting and stopping their arrangement together.
- Give students a few moments to practice improvising several melody options in E minor pentatonic on their recorders. Tell students they'll improvise as a solo in a few moments.
  - **SEL Self-Awareness:** *How might it feel to improvise as a solo? What does it feel like right now before the solo? Musicians can feel many things about a solo performance! What options do we have to add challenges or supports to the improvisation?* (Students might suggest choosing to improvise mostly on low E and G, or to expand their toneset to include more pitches.)
- In their groups, ask students to number off one through four. Tell students this is the order in which they will improvise as a solo.
- Do a whole-class rondo practice by asking each number in the student groups to improvise a melody to their rhythm at the same time. (All *ones* play at the same time, all *twos* play at the same time, etc.)
- Students improvise solos in rondo form. In the A section, all students speak the rhyme while performing a steady beat on body percussion of students' choice. In the contrasting sections, students take turns improvising their melody in E-minor pentatonic in their number order.

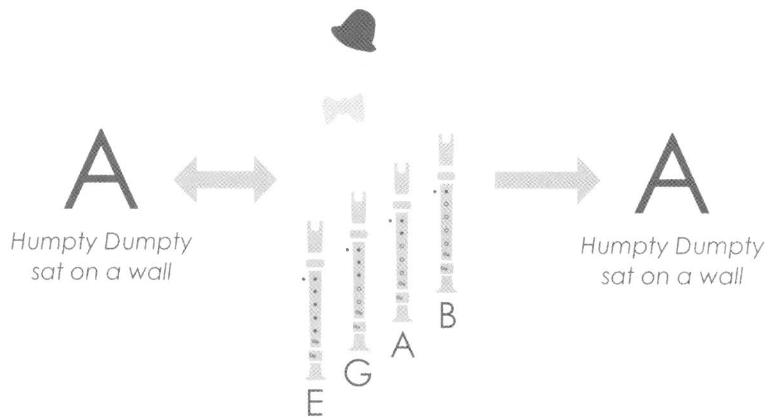

ARRANGING: LOWER ELEMENTARY

Body Percussion Arranging with Steady Beat: Bee Bee Bumblebee

Elimination Game: Students sit in a circle and pass a ball around to a steady beat while speaking the rhyme. The person on whom the beat lands at the end of the rhyme is eliminated.

Arranging Project: Arrange steady beat for body percussion

Preparing the Project:

- Before the project, students should have experience with steady beat. They should also be able to speak "Bee Bee Bumblebee" and play the game without teacher assistance.
- **Teaching the Game:** Speak "Bee Bee Bumblebee" while patting a steady beat with students. Ask questions to refine students' listening (*What happens at the end of the rhyme? What is our rhyme about? What do you think a snout is?*) and repeat the rhyme while patting the steady beat between each question. Lead students in speaking the rhyme through echoing four-beat phrases. Play the game by pointing to students in a steady beat around the circle. When you observe students pointing accurately, add a ball or another small object for students to pass in a steady beat while they speak the rhyme. The person who is "out" plays a steady beat on a tubano or other unpitched percussion instrument.

CLASS 1

Objective: Students perform a steady beat in a class arrangement

The student performs a steady beat in a class arrangement	
4	The student performs a steady beat in a class arrangement with complete accuracy throughout the entire performance
3	The student performs a steady beat in a class arrangement accurately throughout the majority of the performance; some articulations of the beat may be slightly ahead or behind the tempo
2	The student performs an inconsistent steady beat throughout the performance of the class arrangement
1	The student does not perform a steady beat

Materials: "Bee Bee Bumblebee" arranging worksheet, body percussion manipulatives cut into cards

Process:

- Students sit on the ground in a circle. Lead students in speaking the rhyme and playing the game. As the object is passed around the circle, ask all students to pat the steady beat and clap on the word, "out."
  - **SEL Responsible Decision-Making:** *For us to play this game, everyone has to work together to keep the same steady beat. It's how we create a musical team, or "ensemble." When we pass to the steady beat, it's important not to throw the ball or move it too quickly. That helps everyone stay together in our ensemble!*

- After a few rounds, play the game and inner hear the rhyme while patting the steady beat and clapping on the word, "out."
- Motion for students to stand and follow your motions for keeping the steady beat. Use simultaneous imitation, speaking the rhyme and showing the steady beat a variety of ways in four-beat groupings. Students may also offer suggestions for body percussion combinations the class will try.
  - **Adjusting to Assessment Data:** Consider using two levels of body percussion when doing this activity. Observe student performances to assess when the class is ready to move on to other body percussion combinations in four-beat groupings.
- Display the steady beat arrangements on the board and lead students in following the body percussion.

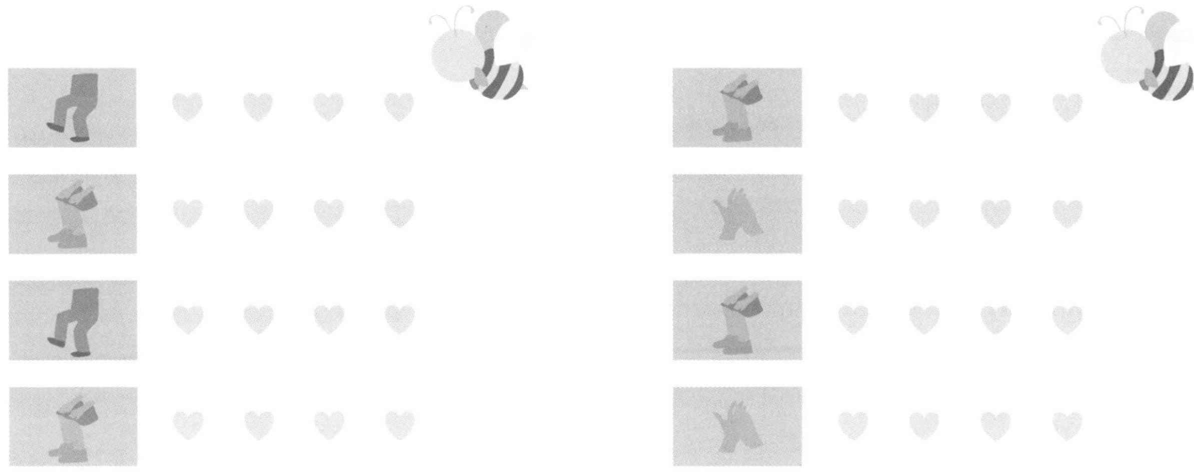

- Create a class arrangement with the "Bee Bee Bumblebee" arranging worksheet and body percussion manipulatives. Place the worksheet on the ground. Ask students to suggest a body percussion level for each row. Place a body percussion icon next to each row of steady beat hearts to show how to keep the steady beat.
- Perform student arrangements as time allows and observe students performing a steady beat to the class arrangement.

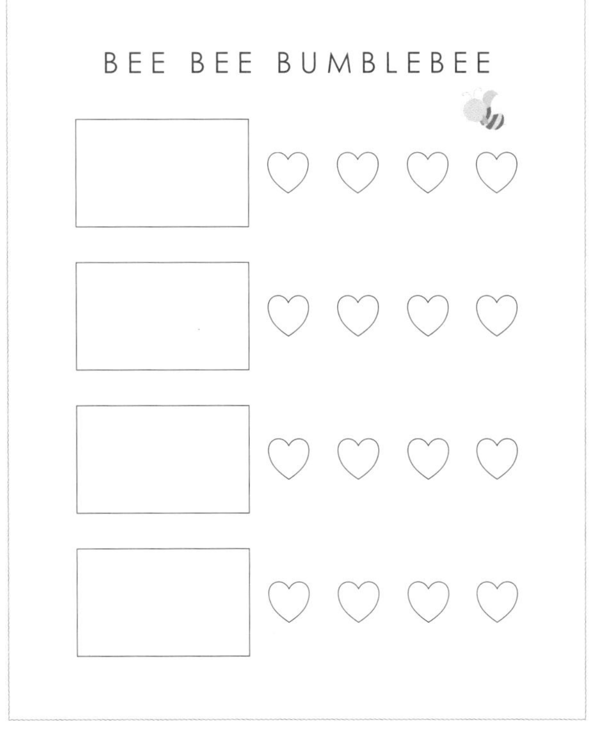

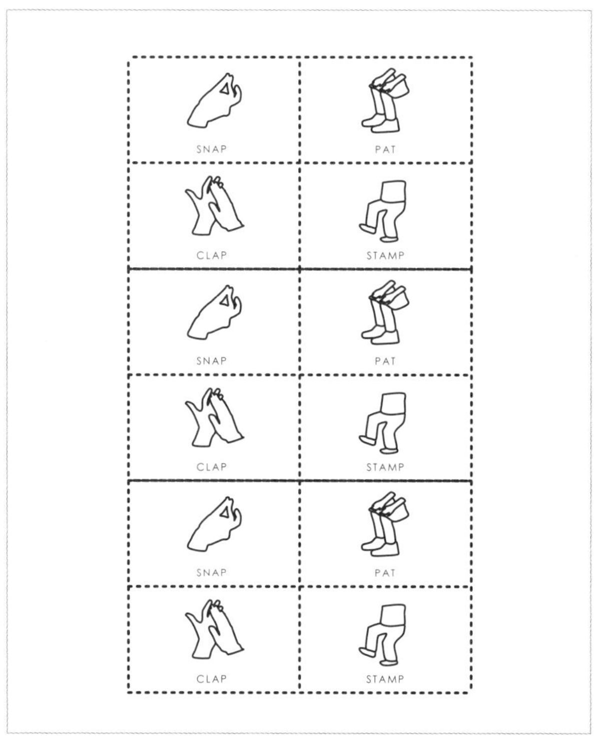

CLASS 2 

Objective: Students arrange the steady beat of "Bee Bee Bumblebee" for body percussion

Assessment:

The student arranges the steady beat of "Bee Bee Bumblebee" for body percussion	
3	The student arranges the steady beat of "Bee Bee Bumblebee" for body percussion
1	The student does not arrange the steady beat of "Bee Bee Bumblebee" for body percussion

Materials: "Bee Bee Bumblebee" arranging worksheet, body percussion manipulatives cut into cards

Process:

- Lead students in speaking the rhyme and playing the game.
- Place the "Bee Bee Bumblebee" Arranging Worksheet on the ground. Review placing the manipulatives next to each row of steady beat hearts.
- Take a student suggestion for the steady beat arrangement and practice performing it as a class.
- After performing the steady beat arrangement, students play the game again.
- As students play the game and pat the steady beat, walk around the outside of the circle and place arranging papers and beat manipulatives behind pairs of students.
- When the rhyme is over, ask students to sit and place their hands on their heads or shoulders as they listen to directions.
- Ask students to create their own arrangement of the steady beat with their shoulder partner using the objects behind them. Tell students they'll share their arrangement in a few moments.
- Give students time to create their arrangement and practice it with their shoulder partner.
  - **SEL Social Awareness:** Both students in the partnership can have "correct" ideas for the arrangement. Encourage students to both contribute to the arrangement and listen to their partner's ideas.
- As students work, walk around the room and narrate the positive behavior you see. *I notice friends trying different ideas; I notice groups that are keeping a steady beat; I hear friends taking turns sharing and listening.* This is also the time to help students check their arrangement. *Does your steady beat performance match what you wrote on the paper? If not, would you like to practice more so your performance matches the paper, or would you like to change what you wrote?*
- After a few moments, do a whole-class practice of student arrangements. Give students a few more moments to practice their arrangements if necessary.
- Divide the class in half. One half of the class performs their arrangement while the other half watches.
- When the arrangement is over, briefly take feedback from the audience. What did students notice about the arrangements they saw?
  - **SEL Social Awareness:** It can be helpful to have a class celebration signal, such as jazz hands or a thumbs up. Help students recognize that when they celebrate their classmates' performances, they're contributing to a classroom environment where everyone's musical voice is celebrated.
- Repeat the activity so both groups of students have the chance to be the audience and the performers.

Rhythmic Building Block Arranging with Ta, Ta-Di, and Ta Rest: All Around the Buttercup

English Counting-Out Rhyme
Melody by Victoria Boler

Arranging Project: Rhythmic Building Block Arranging with *ta, ta-di,* and *ta rest*

Preparing the Project:

- Before the project, students should have conscious knowledge of steady beat, rhythm, rhythm vs beat, quarter notes, beamed eighth notes, and quarter rest. There are adaptations in the activities if students are still working on this vocabulary. They should also be able to sing "All Around the Buttercup" without teacher assistance.
- **Teaching the Song:** Sing the song while students pat a steady beat. Instead of "just pick me," sing the name of a student volunteer to show a new way to keep the steady beat. After several rounds, ask students to sing the first half while you sing the second half. Transition to students singing the whole song without assistance.

CLASS 1

Objective: Students speak an ostinato with *ta, ta-di,* and *ta rest*

Assessment:

The student speaks an ostinato with *ta, ta-di,* and *ta rest*	
4	The student speaks an ostinato with *ta, ta-di,* and *ta rest* with complete accuracy
3	The student speaks an ostinato with *ta, ta-di,* and *ta rest* with accuracy throughout the majority of the performance
2	The student speaks an ostinato with *ta, ta-di,* and *ta rest* with inconsistent accuracy
1	The student speaks an ostinato with *ta, ta-di,* and *ta rest* inaccurately, or does not participate

Materials: Rhythmic building blocks (display set)

Process:

- Sing the song and move around the room in a line with the teacher as the leader. As you move, consider different pathways you might take around the room. Use the three options on the board, or create your own pathway. Students should sing and step a steady beat as they move.

- After a few rounds of the song, invite student leaders to lead the class around the room, stepping in a steady beat and singing without teacher assistance.
- As students walk around the room in their line, go to the board and display the rhythmic building blocks.

- Motion for students to sit in place. Point to the rhythms and speak eight-beat combinations on the syllables of your choice. Students echo.
  - **Flexible Levels of Notational Literacy:** If quarter notes, beamed eighth notes, and quarter rests are unknown vocabulary for your students, they may aurally identify which rhythms have long sounds, short sounds, and no sound. Continue the activity with "short" and "long" icons instead of Standard Western notation. If students have lots of experience with quarter notes, beamed eighth notes, and quarter rests, consider an aural decoding activity. Speak the rhythms on flower names and ask students to speak the rhythms back on rhythm syllables.

- Lay out the rhythmic building blocks (display set) on the ground or on the board. Ask student volunteers to suggest an order of four building blocks. Count the class off to read the new eight-beat arrangement.

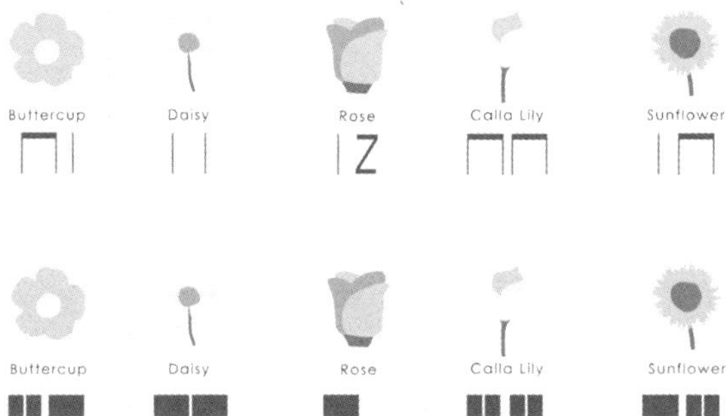

- After reading several eight-beat arrangements ask students to suggest a four-beat ostinato with two cards. Lead students in speaking the ostinato four times in a row.
  - **Example:**

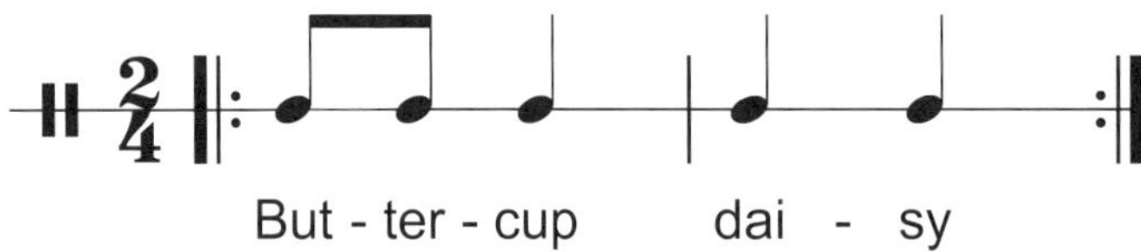

- Students stand in a circle around the building blocks and speak the rhythm while walking in a circle. Sing the song as students speak the ostinato.

CLASS 2

Objective: Students arrange rhythmic building blocks using quarter notes, beamed eighth notes, and quarter rest

Assessment:

The student arranges rhythmic building blocks using *ta*, *ta-di*, and *ta rest*	
3	The student arranges rhythmic building blocks using *ta*, *ta-di*, and *ta rest*
1	The student does not arrange rhythmic building blocks using *ta*, *ta-di*, and *ta rest*

Materials: Rhythmic building blocks (student set)

Process:

- Sing and move around the room, stepping a steady beat in a line with a student as the leader. As students move, they may use one of the movement pathways on the board, or create their own. Listen for students singing the song without assistance and stepping a steady beat.

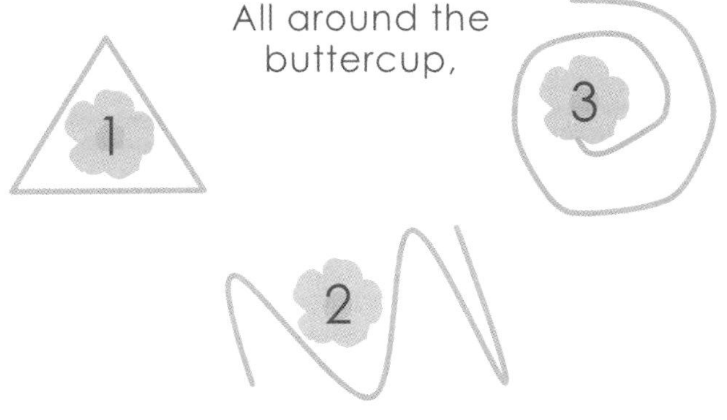

- Divide the class in half, creating two lines. Two student leaders move their line around the room at the same time, making new pathways. Consider adding a chord bordun to keep time as students move:

- After a few rounds of the song, display combinations of rhythmic building blocks on the board. Count students off and practice the new arrangements together.

- When you observe that students speak the rhythms accurately without assistance, ask students to sing the song as they find a partner by making eye contact. Students sit on the ground when they have a partner.
  - **SEL Relationship Skills:** In this activity, students practice using nonverbal communication (eye contact) to find a partner. Consider leading a discussion about what it's like to find a partner nonverbally (eye contact, nodding, etc.) instead of verbally (asking a classmate to be partners). If making eye contact is a challenge, are there other non-verbal supports students might use, such as looking above their classmates' eyes or turning their bodies to face their classmates?
- With their partner, ask students to imagine a new order of the rhythms. As students work in pairs, walk around the room passing out the rhythmic building blocks.
  - **Note:** Students will arrange four blocks, but may use more than one set of cards to give the option of duplicating rhythms.
- Give students a few moments to try out their options and practice performing.
- Ask pairs of students to share their arrangements with the class as time allows.
- After the pair shares, the rest of the class gives a thumbs up, a smile, or jazz hands as a "thank you." Ask students in the audience to share something they noticed about the rhythm they just heard. After a brief time to share observations, ask the students who just performed to choose the next volunteer group.
  - **What Do you Notice?** Encourage students to find similarities and differences in their peers' rhythmic combinations. Some rhythm arrangements will have "twins" in the class (identical arrangements). Some rhythm arrangements might have musical opposites, with the same cards in reverse order. Students might also point out when a group uses a rhythm more than once in their arrangement, or uses all different rhythms. There are many possible observations!

CLASS 3 

Objective: Students perform their arrangements of rhythmic building blocks

Assessment:

The student performs their arrangement of rhythmic building blocks	
4	The student performs their arrangement of rhythmic building blocks with precise rhythmic accuracy and a steady beat throughout the entire performance
3	The student performs their arrangement of rhythmic building blocks with precise rhythmic accuracy and a steady beat throughout the majority of the performance
2	The student performs their arrangement of rhythmic building blocks with inaccuracies in the performance, such as hesitations that interfere with the steady beat
1	The student does not perform an arrangement of rhythmic building blocks

Materials: Rhythmic building blocks (student set)

Process:

- Sing the song and move around the room, stepping a steady beat in a line with a student as the leader. As students move, they may use one of the movement pathways on the board, or create their own.
- Display the rhythmic building blocks on the board.
- Ask students to sing the song as they find a partner by making eye contact and sit on the ground.
  - **SEL Social Awareness:** Encourage students to consider partnering with classmates they have not yet talked with today.
- With their partner, ask students to imagine a new order of the rhythms. As students work in pairs, walk around the room passing out the rhythmic building blocks.
  - **Note:** Students will arrange four blocks, but you might pass out more than one set of cards to give the option of duplicating rhythms.
- Tell students that each group will perform their rhythms as a solo. Give students a few moments to practice performing their arrangement.
  - **SEL Self-Management:** *What do we want our arrangements to sound like? How will we know we've done a good job in our rhythm performance?* Work together as a class to create a small checklist (three to five items) of criteria. Write students' assessment criteria on the board.
  - Sample criteria might be:

    We play our rhythms together
    We keep the same steady beat as the song
    We play our rhythms accurately
- Perform rhythm arrangements in a student-arranged rondo:
- Choose one pair of students to be the rondo leader and the other student in the pair to play a chord bordun to accompany the song.
- The rondo leader walks around the groups, creating a movement pathway while the rest of the class sings the song. At the end of the song, the student leader stops in front of one student group. That group performs their rhythm arrangement and the class echoes. Sing the song again as the leader continues to walk around the students and stop at the next performer group. Continue through several rounds of the rondo, then switch out the leader and the bordun player.

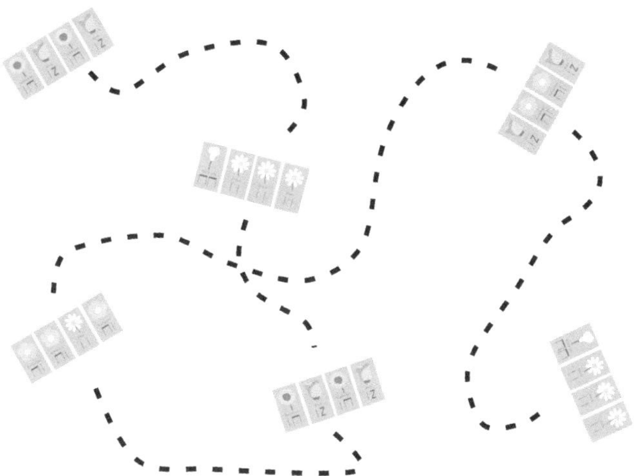

- When each group has performed their rhythm arrangement, ask students to turn to their partner and assess their performance using the criteria on the board.

Extension:

- Consider using this activity at an informance, parent night, or other music sharing event. With written permission from administration and guardians, the activity might also be videoed and shared on the school website.

Barred Instrument Arranging with Do, Re, Mi, Sol: Duerme Pronto

Puerto Rican Lullaby

Translation:

Go to sleep soon dear little child,
Sleep now without crying
You're in the arms of your mother, singing to you.

Arranging Project: Arrange a melody for an existing rhythm

Preparing the Project:

- Before the project, students should have conscious melodic knowledge of *do, re, mi,* and *sol*. They should also be able to sing "Duerme Pronto" without teacher assistance.
- **Teaching the Song:** Sing the song while rocking side to side with students. Ask if there are any words students recognize. What could this song be about? Why do they think that? Are there any words that repeat? Share that this Spanish-language lullaby is from a place in America called Puerto Rico. Show Puerto Rico on the map. Students can connect this lullaby with others they might hear in their homes. Share the translation of the lullaby with students (*Go to sleep my little baby, go to sleep and do not cry*). Notice that "duerme pronto" happens twice in the song. Echo sing "duerme pronto." Lead students in singing "duerme pronto" (measures 1 and 3) without assistance while you sing measures 2 and 4. Eventually transition to students singing the whole song without assistance. Students may sing both verses, or just the first verse for this project.

CLASS 1

Objective: Students create movements that match aaab form

Assessment:

Students create movements that match aaab form	
3	Students create movements that match aaab form
1	Students create movements that do not match aaab form, or do not move

Process:

- Lead students in singing the song and stepping a steady beat in open space.
- Motion for students to sit. Ask them to discuss what they know about the song with someone next to them. (This is a lullaby from a place in America called Puerto Rico. It's sung to help a baby go to sleep. The language is Spanish.)
- After a few moments, motion for students to stand. Ask students to inner hear the song while stepping a steady beat in open space.
- *I've noticed something interesting about this song - how does this song end? Does it move up or down?* (Down.)
- Step in open space and "float" down to the ground at the end of the song.
- Analyze the form: Ask students to sing the song on a "loo" and listen for the parts of the melody (not the words) that match. Identify the form as aaab, or same same same different.
    - **Identifying Form:** Hold up four fingers as students sing (one finger for each phrase). Track each phrase as students sing to help students identify that the first three phrases have the same melody.

- Brainstorm motions to create a class movement arrangement that matches the form of the song. The last four beats will continue to end with a downward motion.
- **Examples:**
  - Students stand in a circle. Float arms outside, then inside the circle three times in a row, then float down down to the ground.
  - Slide slowly to the right three times, then float down to the ground.
  - Rock side to side for the first three phrases, then float down to the ground.
- In groups of two to four, students create movements that match the form of the song.
  - **SEL Relationship Skills:** Some students will have many movement ideas for this arrangement! Some students will have fewer ideas. Encourage everyone in the group to actively take part in the goal by practicing balancing *contributing* ideas with *listening to* ideas.
  - **Motions and Musical Context:** Review that this is a lullaby. *If this is a lullaby, how should we move?* Ask students to consider the context of the song as they create their movements.
- Give students a few moments to practice, then do a whole-class runthrough. Play the melody on recorder or a barred instrument, or sing on a neutral syllable as students perform their movement compositions.

CLASS 2

Objective: Students trace melodic contour to *do, re, mi,* and *sol*

Assessment:

The student traces melodic contour to *do, re, mi,* and *sol*	
3	The student traces melodic contour to *do, re, mi,* and *sol*
1	The student does not trace melodic contour to *do, re, mi,* and *sol*

Process:

- Standing in a circle, lead students in movements that match the form of the song. Ask students to recall what they did in their small groups last class and take student suggestions for the whole-class movement. Continue to use a downward motion for the last phrase.
- Recall that the form of the song is *aaab,* or *same same same different.*
- Ask students to sing the song while walking to their spots.
- Sing questions to aurally identify *mi re do* in the song: *I noticed something about the last three pitches we sing, "sin llorar." Do those pitches move up by step or down by step?* (Down.) Lead students in checking their answer by tracing the melodic contour of "sin llorar." *Does it sound like we landed on the home pitch to end the song, or a different pitch to make the song keep going?* (Home pitch to end the song.) *In this class, what do we call three pitches moving down by step to the home note?* (Mi re do.)
  - **Flexible Levels of Notational Literacy:** If the pitches, *mi re do* are not conscious vocabulary, this can be the time to share the pitch names and hand signs after students aurally identify three pitches moving down by step, ending on the home note.
- Seated in a circle, lead students in tracing the melodic contour of the first three phrases. End with solfege hand signs, singing *mi re do.*
- *Let's change the order of the pitches at the beginning sections of the song to create a new arrangement. We'll keep the rhythm the same. Copy the new melody when you're ready, and we'll all end on* "mi re do" *together.*
- Use simultaneous imitation to explore several different options for a new melodic arrangement. Improvise four beats on a neutral syllable using the pitches from the song (*do, re, mi, sol*) and trace the melodic contour. Students copy the melodic contour motion, then join in when they're comfortable. The whole class ends with "*mi re do.*"

- **Examples:**

- Add a quiet chord bordun. Ask students to imagine their own lullaby in their heads that the class could repeat.
  - **Harmonic Accompaniment:** A chord bordun helps students stay grounded in the tonic pitch for the song. This harmonic accompaniment could also be performed on another classroom instrument, like a guitar or ukulele.
- Ask students to practice their lullaby by humming it and tracing the melodic contour while you play the chord bordun. Sing *mi re do* at the end.
  - **Divergent Melodies:** Any melodic output students create is acceptable at this point in the creative process. Students are not being asked to create melodies using specific solfege syllables. Rather, they'll use the melodic context provided by the song and the bordun accompaniment to create their own melody.
- When students have a melody they like, take student volunteers. And ask them to sing and move to their melody on a neutral syllable. Continue playing the chord bordun quietly as the student shares their melody idea, then lead the class in singing along and ending with *mi re do*. Thank the musician for sharing their song.
  - **SEL Relationship Skills:** *When someone teaches us their song, how should we respond?* Students might articulate that they should listen with musical ears and sing along with the students' song when they're ready. They might also decide to give the student a smile or compliment when the song is over.

CLASS 3

Objective: Students arrange a new melody to an existing rhythm using *do, re, mi,* and *sol.*

Assessment:

The student plays a new melody to an existing rhythm using *do, re, mi,* and *sol*	
3	The student plays a new melody to an existing rhythm using *do, re, mi,* and *sol*
1	The student does not play a new melody to an existing rhythm using *do, re, mi,* and *sol,* or does not perform

Materials: Barred instruments set up in C pentatonic (enough for pairs of students to share)

Process:

- Lead students in singing the song and stepping a steady beat in open space. Tell students you're listening for the song and watching for a gentle steady beat.
- When you observe students stepping in a steady beat and singing the song accurately, tap students on the shoulder or make eye contact and nod. When students are chosen by you, they continue to sing and step a steady beat as they move to stand behind an instrument. Continue until there are two students behind each instrument.
  - **Moving to Barred Instruments:** If this process is new to your students, consider showing the steps to walk to a barred instrument safely and musically. Demonstrate your expectation by stepping a steady beat and singing the song as you move to stand behind an instrument. Ask a few students at a time to demonstrate moving to the barred instruments safely and musically. Transition to all students walking safely and musically behind a barred instrument and celebrate student success with jazz hands.
- At barred instruments, students work with their partner to find the pitches the song uses: *do, re, mi,* and *sol,* with *do* on C. Notice that there are two sets of these pitches on the instrument, a low set and a high set. Students may choose which octave to play in.

- Invite students to work with their partner to figure out the song by ear. Give students a few moments to work, then play the song together as a class.
- Ask students to imagine a new order to the first four beats of the song. Give students time to experiment with their melody arrangements. Remind students that they'll repeat their new idea three times in a row, since the form of the song is *aaab*, or *same same same different*. All arrangements will end with *mi re do*.
  - **SEL Relationship Skills:** Encourage students to take turns sharing the mallets without a specific teacher prompt. Let students know the amount of time they have to explore a new melody (about two or three minutes) and set the expectation that both students have at least one chance to play the instrument.
- Ask students to check their work with a whole-class run-through. Lead students in playing their new arrangements of the melody two times so both partners have a chance to play. The partner who does not have mallets may choose to sing the arrangement on "loo" or tap the arrangement on another octave of the instrument.

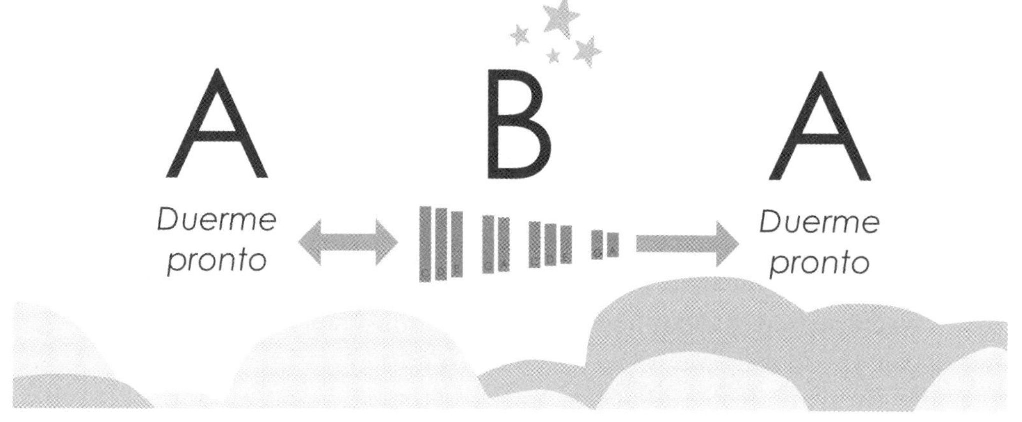

- When students are ready, invite them to share their arrangements in a rondo. Sing the song as the A section. As students sing in the A section, make eye contact and smile with a student as the signal for them to share their arrangement. The partner who does not have mallets may choose to sing the arrangement on "loo" or tap the arrangement on another octave of the instrument. All students sing the A section again while you make eye contact and smile with the next performers.
- At the end of the rondo, thank the students who shared their songs.

CLASS 4

Objective: Students perform an arrangement in rondo form

Assessment:

The student performs their part of the arrangement in rondo form	
3	The student performs their part of the arrangement in rondo form
1	The student does not perform their part of the arrangement in rondo form

Materials: Barred instruments set up in C pentatonic (enough for pairs of students to share), maracas (optional)

- Standing in a circle, lead students in movements that match the form of the song. Ask students to recall what they did in their small groups in a previous class and take student suggestions for the whole-class movement.
- Motion for students to sit. Review that the song is a lullaby from Puerto Rico. What might you say if you were trying to get a baby to go to sleep? Ask students to think their idea in their head and share it with their shoulder partner.
- Take student suggestions. When students share their idea, lead the class in whispering the phrase in simple meter as they pat a steady beat.
  - **Examples:**

- Choose a student suggestion that has a complimentary rhythm to the song.
  - The complementary ostinato will have a rhythm that is not identical to the rhythm of the melody.
- Ask students to whisper the ostinato while patting a steady beat as you sing the song, then divide the class in half. One half sings the song and pats a steady beat. The other half whispers the ostinato while patting a steady beat.
  - **Partwork Interdependence:** If students struggle to maintain the ostinato, ask them to speak the pattern four times in a row while patting the steady beat without teacher assistance. Remind students that they should listen to each other to stay together. When students successfully perform the ostinato on their own without help, sing the song quietly while still encouraging the class to listen to each other. Gradually add students on your "team" to sing the song until the class is divided in half.
- *We've done so many musical things with this song! Let's see if we can put it all together in our very own class arrangement.*
- As a class, develop a list of musical experiences students have explored in the past several lesson segments:
  - Singing the song
  - Playing student arrangements of the song on barred instruments
  - Moving to the form of the song in small groups
  - Whispering an ostinato students created
  - **Thinking About Creativity:** It can be helpful to point out to students that they have created three out of the four elements on the board. The teacher presents the song. The students create the melodic arrangement, the movement, and the ostinato.
- Tell students that just like last class, everyone sings the song during the A section. Then, students take turns sharing their arrangements of the melody. Notice that there are two elements not included in the song: the movement and the ostinato.

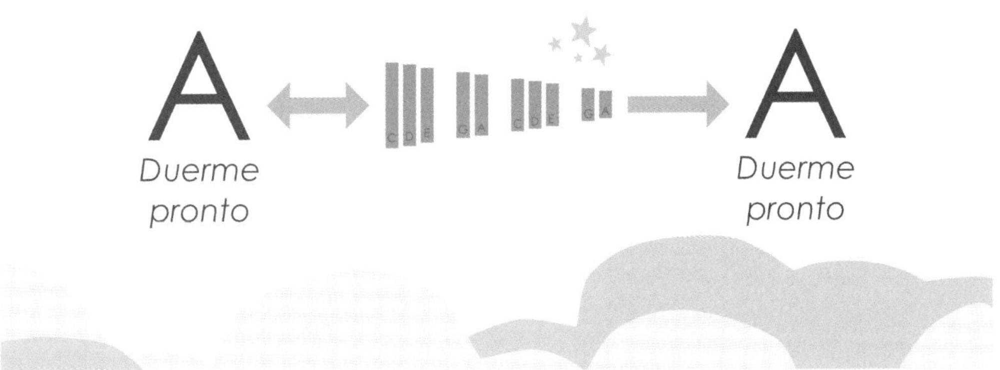

- *Should we do movements during the singing or during the barred instrument melodies?* Vote as a class.
- *Should we do the ostinato during the singing or during the barred instrument melodies?* Vote as a class.
- Ask students to think about their preference for playing their barred instrument melody, speaking the ostinato, and moving in a small group. Ask students to hold up one, two, or three fingers to show their preference as you call out the different options.
  - **SEL Social Awareness:** What does it mean to be in a musical ensemble? When we get our second preference instead of our first preference, how can we react? It's okay to be disappointed while doing your best at the musical job you have.
- Divide students into three groups, taking student preference into account when making the decisions.
  - **Dividing the Ensemble:** There are many options for dividing students into ensemble groups! The choice you make will depend on your students' experience with independent small-group work and your comfort level working with several musical groups at once. To add support for classroom

management, only choose a small number of students to play barred instruments and the ostinato. Those students practice independently as you work with the rest of the class in the movement group. To add more complexity, divide the class into groups more evenly.

- Give students a few moments to review their parts in their groups. Students at a barred instrument may recall their previous melody or create a new melody. Students in the moving group will create movements in aaab form, either as a group or in smaller groups of two to four students. Students who speak the ostinato might transfer their rhythm to maracas.
- Perform the student arrangement in rondo form. With written permission from administration and student guardians, consider videoing the performance to share.

ARRANGING: UPPER ELEMENTARY

Barred Instrument Arranging with Low La: Old Mister Rabbit

Chasing Game (by Victoria Boler)

- **Players** - Cabbage, Farmer, Rabbit
- Choose one student to be the cabbage. The cabbage stands on one side of the room with palms up, ready to be tagged. The rest of the class stands in a circle. Choose one student from the circle to be the farmer. Choose another student from the circle secretly to be the rabbit.
- All students walk in a circle to a steady beat while singing the song. At the end of the song, the rabbit runs to tag the cabbage and the farmer runs to tag the rabbit. The rabbit must get to the cabbage before being tagged by the farmer.

Arranging Project: Add a melody to rhythmic building blocks

Preparing the Project:

- Before the project, students should have conscious knowledge of *do*, *re*, *mi*, and experience with *low la*. They should also be able to sing the song and play the game to "Old Mister Rabbit" without assistance. The project rhythmic building blocks use quarter notes, eighth notes, and quarter rests. Students may speak these rhythms on rhythm syllables or on food names.
- **Teaching the Song:** Sing the song while leading students in patting a steady beat. Who are the characters in the song? What do they want? Ask students to sing the second half while you continue to sing the first half. Add the game. After a few rounds of the game, students sing the song without teacher assistance.

CLASS 1

Objective: Students improvise with *low la*

The student improvises with *low la*	
3	The student improvises with *low la*
1	The student does not improvise with *low la*, or does not improvise

Materials: Barred instruments set up in F pentatonic (enough for students to share)

Process:

- Lead students in singing the song and playing the game.
- Motion for students to sing the song as they move back their spots.
- With students seated, display the rhythmic building blocks: cabbage, sweet potato, corn, bell pepper, artichoke.

- Ask student volunteers to choose four cards. The volunteer musician leads the class in an eight-beat rhythmic improvisation. The class echoes on body percussion of their choice.
- To switch turns, the student improviser makes eye contact with another musician in the circle when the class echoes. That musician improvises the next combination of text and the class echoes with body percussion of their choice.
  - **Levels of Choice in Improvisation:** If students have limited experience with text improvisation, ask them to choose two rhythmic building blocks to create their eight beats.
  - **Examples:**

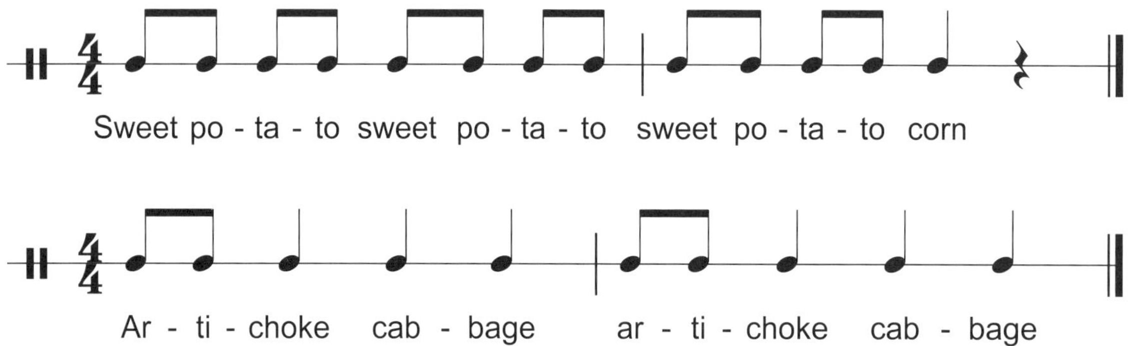

- Display the text of the song on the board.

- Ask students to identify the lowest pitch in the song by holding up one, two, or three fingers. (The correct answer is three.)
- Use a barred instrument set up in F pentatonic and ask, If *do* is F right now, where is the pitch that is lower than *do*? Lead students to identify that the low pitch is a skip below *do* (F) on D.
  - **Flexible Levels of Notational Literacy:** If *low la* is conscious vocabulary for students, the activity can be done with students identifying *low la*. If *low la* is not conscious vocabulary, students can aurally identify a skip lower than the tonic pitch, *do*. Students do not need to consciously know the element to use it in their improvisation.

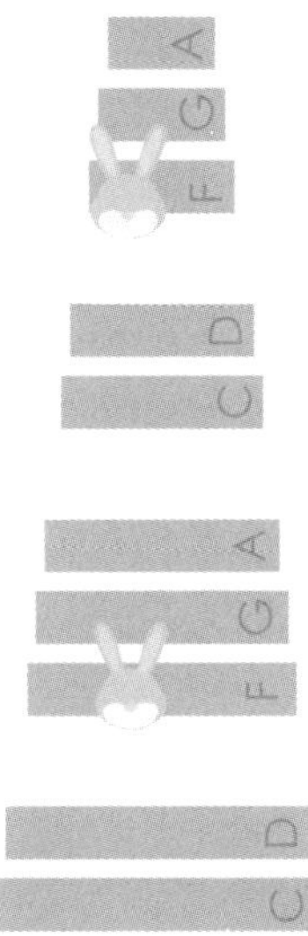

- Create a circle with barred instruments.
  - **Flexible Instrumentation:** If you have access to the instrumentation, each student may have an instrument. Students may also sit with two musicians behind one instrument, each playing on one octave. With limited instruments, create a small circle and have students sit in lines behind the players, then move up when it's their turn to play.
- Seated behind a barred instrument, give students a few moments to identify *do, re, mi,* and *low la* with F as *do*. Students may notice there are two possible octaves on the instrument for this activity. They may choose which one they'll play.
- Ask a student volunteer to speak an improvisation using the rhythms on the board. Students echo on F. (Any student not at an instrument may play body percussion)
- Ask another student to speak an eight-beat rhythm improvisation using the rhythms on the board. Students echo on any combination of *do, re, mi,* or *low la*. Continue as time allows, switching players on the barred instruments. (Any student not at an instrument may play body percussion.)
  - **Making Musical Choices:** Ask students to experiment with their improvisations - what happens if they mostly use the low pitch, D? What happens if they mostly use *do*, or F? Which sound do they prefer?

CLASS 2 

Objective: Students write down their melody using *low la*

Assessment:

The student writes down their melody using *low la*	
3	The student writes down their melody using *low la*
1	The student does not write down their melody using *low la*

Process:

- Lead students in singing the song and playing the game.
- Use a barred instrument visual to review the placement of *do*, *re*, *mi*, and the low pitch with F as *do*.
  - **Flexible Levels of Notational Literacy:** If *low la* is an unknown pitch for students, they may aurally identify which pitch in the song is lower than the home pitch, *do*. When students identify this low pitch, label it as *low la*. *If* do *lives on F, what bar is a skip below F?* (D.) *In this class, what do we call the pitch a skip below* do? (Low la.) *If* do *lives on F, where is* low la? (D.)

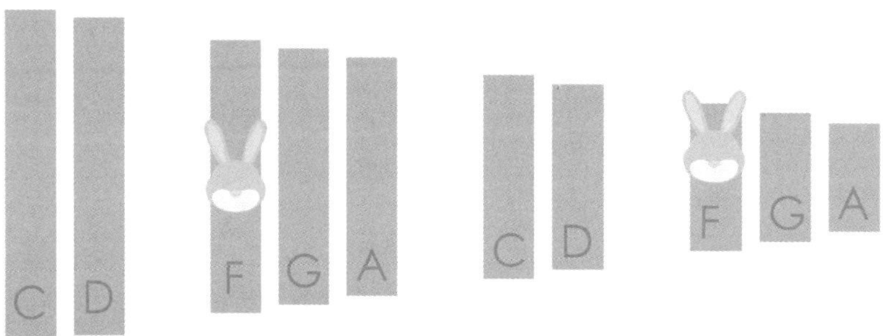

- With their partner, students move to a barred instrument and explore playing the pitches used in this arrangement. After a few moments, review the bars with improvisation:

  - Continue through the pitches used in the song: *do* (F), *re* (G), *mi* (A), and *low la* (low D).
  - Students should recognize that there are two sets of pitches on the instrument. They may choose the octave they'll use to play.
- Tell students the melody of "Old Mister Rabbit" starts on *do*. Give students a few moments to figure out the melody of the song on their instruments by ear.
- As students figure out the melody by ear, walk around the room, passing out the arranging worksheets and pencils. When the worksheets and pencils are passed out, do a whole-class runthrough of the song.
- Show an example of a completed arranging worksheet, front and back. Tell students that later in the class they'll add a melody to their rhythm arrangement and write it down using solfege or letter names. Next class, they'll write their melody on the staff.

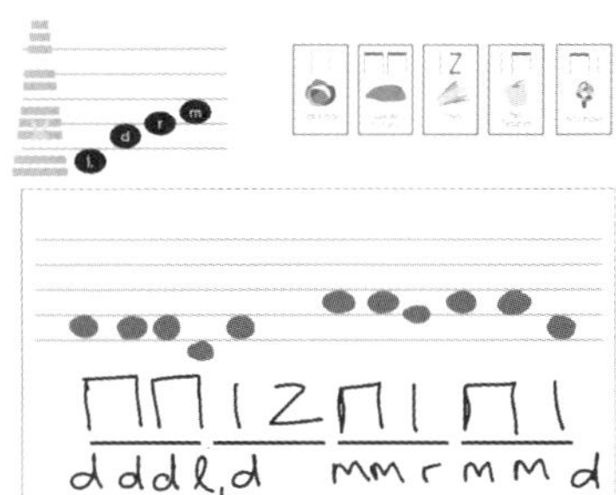

- Display the rhythmic building blocks on the board.

Create an order of four rhythmic building blocks.

Add a melody using *do*, *re*, *mi*, and *low la*.

Play your melody arrangement.

Write down your melody arrangement.

- With a partner, students experiment with an order of rhythmic building blocks.
- When they have an order they like, ask students to add a melody to their rhythmic building block arrangement using *low la*, *do*, *re*, and *mi*. Both partners should be able to play the melodic arrangement.

  ❙ **SEL Social Awareness:** *Why is it important for both partners to be able to play the melody?*
- After students have a melody they like and that both students can play, ask students to write it down on the front of the worksheet. Students may write their melody on solfege or with letter names.
- Ask both partners to point to their names at the top of their paper. One partner turns in the papers and pencils while the other puts away the barred instrument.

CLASS 3

Objective: Notate a melody to rhythmic building blocks

Assessment:

The student notates a melody to rhythmic building block arrangement	
4	The student writes the entire melody on the five-line staff; all noteheads are written clearly on the appropriate lines and spaces
3	The student writes the melody on the five-line staff; a few noteheads are written approximately on the appropriate lines and spaces
2	The student writes notation on the five-line staff; noteheads are written inaccurately on the lines and spaces
1	The student writes illegibly on the five-line staff; or does not write

Materials: Arranging worksheet and pencils, barred instruments set up in F pentatonic (enough for students to share)

Process:

- Students sit with their partner. Show students an example of a completed arranging worksheet.
  - **Flexible Levels of Notational Literacy:** You may show students the worksheet with the appropriate notation level for their development. If students are not ready to write their melodies on the five-line staff, they may write their melodies in graphic notation instead. If students have plenty of practice writing melodies on the staff, they may add stick notation to their melody as well. If necessary, take a few moments to review steps and skips on the staff, and to establish expectations for neatness and legibility.

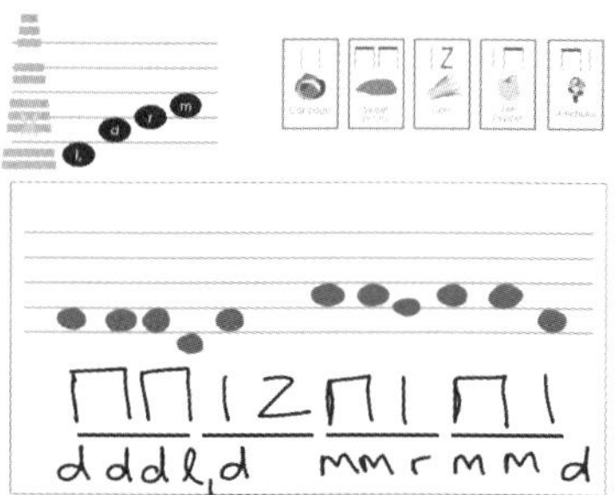

- Ask pairs of students to decide who will get the worksheets and pencils, and who will get the barred instrument for their group, and to give a thumbs up when they have their choice.
- When you observe that students are ready, ask pairs of students at a time to move and get set up.
- Give students time to practice their melody and then write it down.
  - **SEL Self-Management:** Musicians can encounter obstacles when they preserve their work. If students get stuck in the notation process, what should they do? What guides (like their graphic, solfege, or letter name notation, staff names on the worksheet, barred instrument visual, other peers) should they utilize? When should they ask for help from you?
- After several moments, do a whole-class runthrough of students' melodies. Ask students to double-check that the melody they created matches the melody they wrote. If there is a discrepancy, would they like to change the notation to match the melody, or change what they're playing to match the notation? Use a checklist on the board to help students check their work.

- Let's double-check:
  - What I play matches what I wrote
  - Both partners can play the melody
  - The melody is written neatly on the worksheet so someone else can read it
- When you observe students are ready, ask them to pair with another group. Pairs of students take turns teaching their melody to the new group using a combination of rote teaching and notation. Use a class signal (like a bell or hand sign) to show when groups should switch teaching.
  - **SEL Social Awareness:** This is a good time for students to practice how to listen to peers, how to communicate respectfully, and how to give constructive feedback.

Extension:

- This activity could be replicated using recorders instead of barred instruments.

Play Party Arranging with High Do: Tideo

Play Party:

- **Formation:** Create two concentric circles, with each student facing a partner
- 1st half of the song (m. 1 - 8)
  - "Pass" - the outside circle passes one person to the right, so they are facing a new partner
  - "Tideo" - pat, clap, clap partners hands
  - "Jingle at the window" - pat the rhythm of the words
- 2nd half of the song (m. 9 - 16)
  - "Tideo, Tideo" (m. 9 - 10 / m. 13 - 14) - partners switch places so the inside circle is on the outside and the outside circle is on the inside.
  - "Jingle at the window" - pat the rhythm of the words
  - "Tideo" (m. 12 / m. 16) - pat, clap, clap partners hands

Arranging Project: Create a class arrangement of a play party

Preparing the Project:

- Before the project, students should have conscious melodic knowledge of *do, re, mi, sol, la,* and experience with *high do.* They should also be able to sing the song and perform the play party to Tideo.

Teaching the Song Through the Game:

- All students stand in a single circle.
- Students perform simultaneous imitation while the teacher whistles the melody and performs a modified version of the play party.
- In the first half of the song: "Pass" - take one step to the right. "Tideo" - pat, clap, and clap out to an invisible partner. "Jingle at the window" - pat the rhythm of the words.
- In the second half of the song: "Tideo, Tideo" - turn in a circle. "Jingle at the window" - pat the rhythm of the words. "Tideo" - pat, clap, and clap out to an invisible partner.

- Repeat the activity, but sing the text. *How do the words of the song help us know when to move?*
- Sing the song again as students listen and move, then take answers.
- Transition to students performing the traditional play party in concentric circles as they sing the first half of the song.
- Later, students sing the whole song while performing the play party.

CLASS 1

Objective: Students toss a bean bag on the highest pitch of the song in their play party arrangement

Assessment:

The student tosses the bean bag on the highest pitch of the song in their play party arrangement	
3	The student tosses the bean bag on the highest pitch of the song in their play party arrangement
1	The student does not toss the bean bag on the highest pitch of the song in their play party arrangement, or does not participate

Materials: Bean bags (enough for each student to have one)

Process:

- Lead students in singing the song and performing the play party one time.
- *When we switch places with our partner in the second half of the song, we're singing "tideo" but the melody sounds different. How is it different?* Perform the play party again and motion for students to talk to their partner.
- Take answers. (Answers may be divergent - the "tideo" where students switch places has a higher pitch than the rest.)
- Motion for students to sit. *What if we made a new version of the game ourselves instead of playing the one I taught you? Let's make a passing game using bean bags.*
- Tell students that the game they create should be safe and musical. The only other musical rule is that the bean bag should be in the air on the highest pitch of the song. Students will share their arrangements at the end of the lesson segment.
  - **SEL Self-Management:** It can be so fun to use things like bean bags in music class! Musicians use self-management when they collaborate so their final musical product is a good reflection of their group ideas. This means they practice thinking about their emotions and behaviors before acting.
- Ask students to get into groups of four or five and brainstorm their new game ideas. Notice that the lyrics of the song give hints about when to pass. Are there any other game clues hidden in the song lyrics that students might use?
- As students brainstorm, walk around the room giving each student a bean bag.
- Give students several moments to create and practice a new arrangement of the game. Check in with students periodically to see if they're ready to try their arrangement in a practice performance.
  - **SEL Self-Management:** When you check in with students, ask them to show on their fingers how many more minutes their group needs to complete their arrangement.
- When students show they're ready, ask them to double-check with their group that their bean bag is in the air on the highest pitches in the song. Do a whole-class practice run with everyone singing the song and performing their new version of the game.
- Identify that the highest pitches are in the second half of the song, on the words, "tideo tideo."
- Students self-assess their version of the play party with a thumbs up if they threw the bean bag on the highest pitches, a thumbs down if they did not throw the bean bag on the highest pitches, and a sideways thumb if they're not sure.
- Student groups share their arrangement with the class as time allows.
- Ask students to sing the song as they put the bean bags away.

CLASS 2

Objective: Arrange a melodic ostinato using *high do*

Assessment:

The student arranges a melodic ostinato using *high do*	
1	The student arranges a melodic ostinato using *high do*
3	The student arranges a melodic ostinato that does not use *high do*, or does not participate

Materials: Bean bags (enough for each student to have one), barred instruments set up in C pentatonic (enough for students to share)

Process:

- Lead students in singing the song and performing the play party.
- Ask students to get into their groups from the last class and review their arrangement of the passing game. Tell students that they'll make decisions today about an arrangement of the song they'll perform next class. With a few student volunteers, pass out bean bags.
- Give students a few moments to recall their arrangement. When you observe that students are ready, do a whole-class practice of students' new versions.
- Identify that the highest pitches are *high do*, which happen in the second half of the song in the last syllable of "tideo."
    - **Flexible Levels of Notational Literacy:** If *high do* is not a consciously known melodic element, students can identify that the highest pitches happen four times in the second half of the song, in the last syllable of "tideo." Label this pitch as *high do*.
- Lead students in singing the second half of the song on solfege. Give students their starting solfege pitch by pointing to it on a tone ladder, then sing four beats at a time on a neutral syllable. Students sing back on solfege syllables.

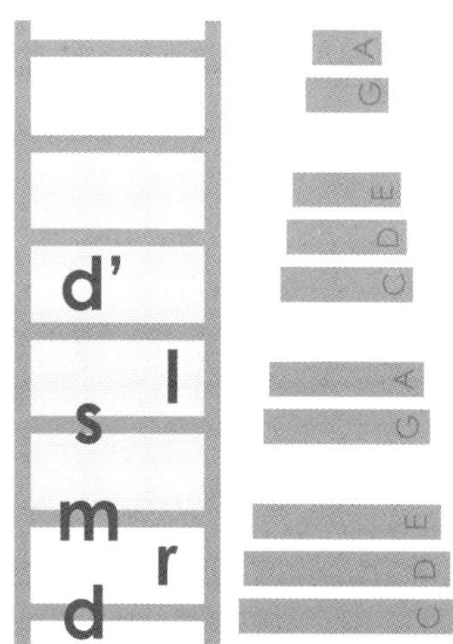

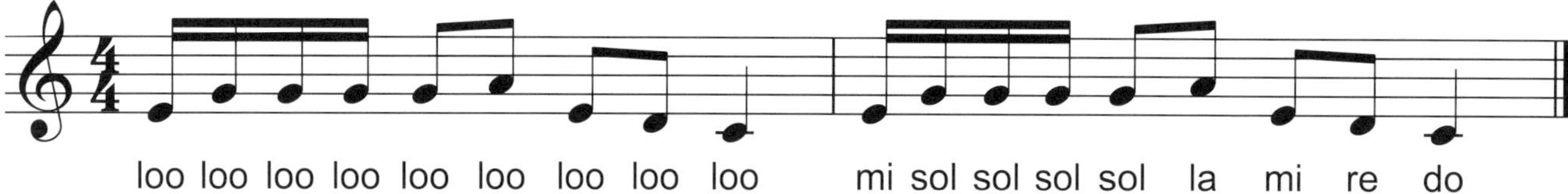

- With a barred instrument visual, review the placement of *do, mi, sol,* and *high do* if C is *do*.
- Ask two students from each group to each get a barred instrument and bring it back to their work area.
- Sharing the instruments in the group, ask students to arrange a melody to the four-beat ostinato using "pass pass" and "jingle at the window" (or "*ta ta*" and "*takadimi ta-di*"). Ask students to use any combination of *do, mi, sol,* and *high do* in their ostinato. They should use *high do* at least one time.
- Give students time to work on their ideas in their groups, and emphasize that each member of the group should be able to play the ostinato four times in a row.
  - Possible answers:

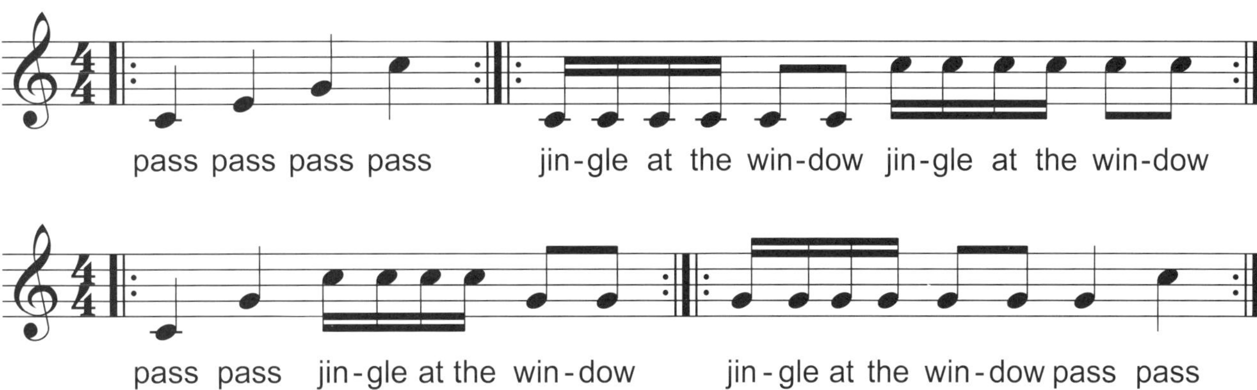

- Check in with students to see if they're ready to try their arrangement in a practice performance. When you check in with students, ask them to show on their fingers how many more minutes their group needs to complete their arrangement.
- When students are ready, do a whole class runthrough, with students playing their ostinato four times in a row. As students perform, add a chord bordun on a barred instrument to keep time. Repeat the activity so the other students in the group get a chance to play.
- Invite students from each group to share their melodic ostinato ideas as the rest of the class sings the song. (Notice that students will need to play their ostinato eight times total to match the length of the song.) After students perform, thank them for sharing.
- Ask students to share their feedback about the ostinati they heard.
  - **SEL Social Awareness:** Musicians can practice valuing the feelings of others when giving feedback. Encourage students to state their preference for the melodic ostinato by referencing the musical work itself, and not referring to it by its creators' names. For example: "I liked that one used *takadimi* three times in a row" instead of "I liked the one created by Davin's group."

CLASS 3

Objective: Students perform an arrangement of "Tideo"

Assessment:

The student performs an arrangement of "Tideo"	
3	The student performs an arrangement of "Tideo"
1	The student does not perform an arrangement of "Tideo"

Materials: Bean bags (enough for each student to have one)

Process:

- Review the elements from previous classes: *We've done a lot of musical things with this song! Let's see if we can put it all together in a class arrangement.*

- As a class, develop a list of musical experiences students have explored in the past several lesson segments:
  - Singing the song
  - Performing the original play party
  - Performing the student arrangement of the play party
  - Playing the student-created ostinati
- Work as a class to combine the elements into a class arrangement. There are many possibilities! Here are a few to consider:
  - **Option 1:**
    - Formation: Students stand in concentric circles. Bean bags and barred instruments are in place for students to return to after the A section.
    - A - Students sing the song and perform the original play party while one person from each group plays their ostinato on a barred instrument.
    - (Interlude) - the ostinato continues as students move to their small groups
    - B - Students perform their version of the play party.
  - **Option 2:**
    - Formation: Four barred instrument players sit at the front of the class. The rest of the class is in their groups with bean bags.
    - A - Four ostinati layer in one measure at a time.
    - B - All students perform their version of the game
    - A - The ostinati layer back out in reverse order.
  - **Option 3:**
    - Formation: Four barred instrument players sit at the front of the class. The rest of the class is in their groups with bean bags, ready to perform in rondo form.
    - A - The ostinato players perform their ostinati four times in a row
    - B / C / D / E, etc. - Student groups take turns sharing their version of the game.
- When students have their idea for the arrangement, consider how they'll know they've done a good job in the performance. Develop a short list of criteria (three to four items).
  - **SEL Self-Management:** *What do we want our arrangements to sound like? How will we know we've done a good job in our performance?* Work together as a class to create a small checklist (three to five items) of criteria. Write students' assessment criteria on the board.
  - Sample criteria might be:
    We stay together as a class
    We remember what sections of the arrangement come next
    We perform our play party arrangement accurately
- Perform the arrangement and lead students through their assessment of the performance.

Extensions:

- Perform student arrangements of the play party in a two-beat round.
- Consider adding an bordun as a time-keeper.

COMPOSITION: LOWER ELEMENTARY

Loud and Quiet Compositions: Grizzly Bear

Game: Students stand in a circle with one person (the grizzly bear) pretending to sleep in the middle. All students step in a steady beat around the bear while singing the song. In the second half of the song, "please be very quiet," student stand still and place their index finger to their lips as they sing. At, "if you wake them," students gradually sing louder and louder and roar at the end of the song. When the class roars, the bear in the middle stands up and chases students. Whoever the bear catches is the next bear and the game begins again.

Composing Project: Students compose with loud and quiet

Preparing the Project:

- Before the project, students should have experience with loud and quiet. They should also be familiar with the song and game to "Grizzly Bear."
- **Teaching the Song:** Students step in a circle to a steady beat and listen to the song. Ask questions: *What is our song about? What do you think the bear is doing?* Add a modified version of the game. All students step in a circle around one student pretending to be the sleeping bear. At the end of the game, all students roar. The bear points to their replacement (instead of chasing) and the game begins again. After several rounds of the game, ask students to sing the second half of the song, "please be very quiet." Eventually transition to students singing the whole song without assistance.

CLASS 1

Objective: Students sing "Grizzly Bear" using an appropriate loud and quiet voice

Assessment:

The student sings "Grizzly Bear" with an appropriate loud and quiet voice	
4	The student uses an appropriate loud or quiet voice through the entire performance
3	The student uses an appropriate loud or quiet voice through most of the performance
2	The student uses an appropriate loud or quiet voice inconsistently through the performance
1	The student uses an inappropriate loud or quiet voice, or does not perform

Process:

- Lead students in singing the song and playing the game.

- **SEL Self-Management:** *It is so fun to play chasing games in music! When musicians work in an ensemble, they use self-management to think about their behaviors and emotions before they act. Let's practice self-management together while we're having so much fun in our chasing game!*

- Seated, lead students in singing the song and patting the steady beat. All students roar at the end.
- *Which part of our game is the quiet part?* (The singing at the beginning.) *Which part of our game is the loud part?* (The second half and the roar at the end.)
- Explore loud and quiet sounds a bear can make - roar, growl, huff, snoring, snarl, etc. Add large and small movements to reflect the big or little dynamic level. Students take turns sharing a loud or quiet sound and movement, and the class echoes.
  - Explore with different types of expression, such as growling with a long, sustained sound, or growling with a short sound. Explore many types of movement expressions, such as making a small tall shape or a large low shape.
- Explore the loud and quiet sounds the person might make in the game - *gasp, sshhhh, whimper, yell*, etc.
- Students take turns sharing a loud or quiet sound and movement, and the class echoes.

CLASS 2

Objective: Students perform a loud and quiet composition with the appropriate voice

Assessment:

The student performs a loud and quiet composition with the appropriate voice	
4	The student performs a loud and quiet composition with the appropriate voice through the entire performance
3	The student performs a loud and quiet composition with the appropriate voice through most of the performance
2	The student performs a loud and quiet composition with the appropriate voice inconsistently through the performance
1	The student performs a loud and quiet composition with an inappropriate voice, or does not perform

Process:

- Lead students in singing the song and playing the game.
- Review vocal explorations from last class (roar, growl, huff, snoring, gasp, sshhhh, whimper, yell, etc.).
- Create a composition with the vocal explorations and lead how students should share: Students will think a musical idea and practice it by inner hearing. Next, students will describe their composition and preserve it by sharing it with the class. The class echoes.
- Demonstrate several examples for the class:

- *This time I'll do loud, then quiet, then loud: ROOOOAAAARRRR grrrr ROOOAAARRR.* Motion for the class to echo.
- *Now I'll do quiet quiet quiet: Grrrr grrrr ssshhhhhhhhhhhh.* Motion for the class to echo.
- *This time I'll do quiet quiet loud: (snore) (snore) AAAAHHHHH!!* Motion for the class to echo.

- *Who has an idea for loud and quiet noises we could make? Think your idea and hold it tightly in your head! When you have your idea ready, please show a quiet thumbs up.*
- Ask student volunteers to speak their composition's order of loud and quiet and preserve it by sharing it with the class. Motion for the class to echo.
  - **SEL Self-Awareness:** *What kinds of sounds are the most fun for you to make? Do you prefer to create loud sounds, quiet sounds, or in-between sounds?*
- Continue with several volunteers. The musician who just shared chooses the next musician.
  - If students share a vocal exploration that does not match how they described the composition, use the appropriate description when you thank them for sharing. For example, "Thank you for sharing your loud composition! Who is showing that they're ready for you to choose them next?"
- Lead students in singing and playing the game to end.

CLASS 3

Objective: Students notate their composition

Assessment:

The student notates their loud and quiet composition	
3	The student notates their loud and quiet composition
1	The student does not notate a loud and quiet composition

Materials: "Grizzly Bear" loud and quiet composition worksheet

Process:

- Lead students in singing the song and playing the game.
- Review the previous class: *Who has an idea for loud and quiet noises we could make? Think your idea and hold it tightly in your head! When you have your idea ready, please show a quiet thumbs up.*
- Ask student volunteers to talk about their composition's order of loud and quiet and then share it with the class. Motion for the class to echo and continue with several volunteers. The musician who just shared chooses the next musician.
- *I'm having trouble remembering everyone's compositions! Let's find a way to write down our big loud sounds and small quiet sounds.*
  - **Graphic Notation for Loud and Quiet:** In the same way that we used big and small movements to show big and small dynamic levels in the first class, young composers can use big and small graphics to notate their composition.

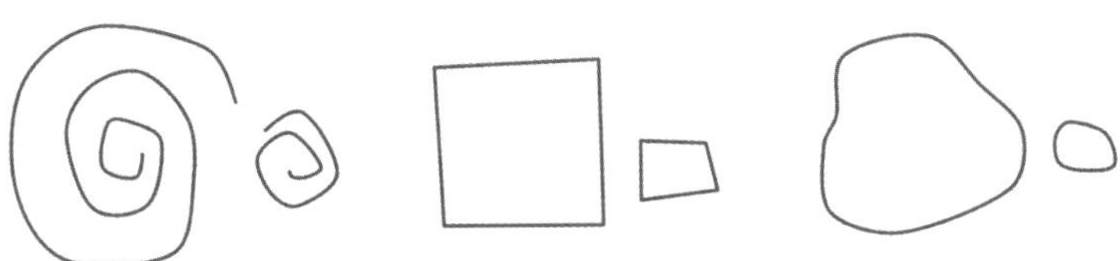

- After the next musician shares their loud and quiet composition and the class echoes, ask the student to come to the board and draw large or small icons to show their sounds.

- Sample notation of a loud loud quiet quiet composition:

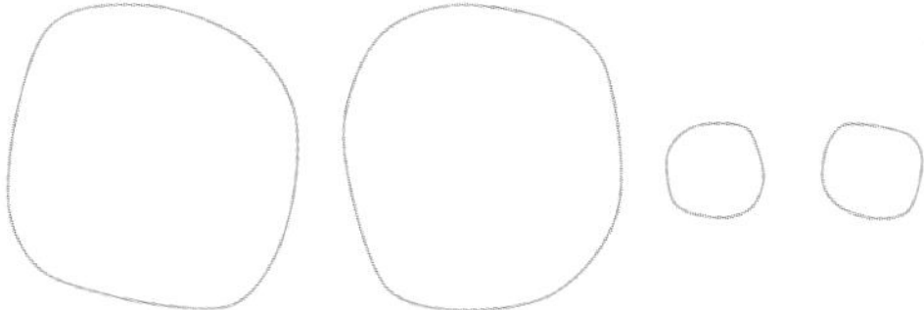

- Sample notation of a quiet loud composition:

- Students take turns sharing their loud and quiet song ideas, and then drawing them on the board.
- Tell students they're about to write down their loud and quiet ideas on paper. Students may use any big and little shapes they want to show their loud and quiet song.
- As students work, walk around the room and encourage students to double-check their work by making sure the big and little sounds they wrote on the page match the order of loud and quiet sounds they hear in their heads.
- After a few moments, invite a student volunteer to come to the front of the room and share their dynamic composition. The class echoes the student, who calls on the next musician to share.

- **SEL Social Awareness:** What are the classroom expectations for sharing a creative work? What should students do before, during, and after their music friend shares their musical idea? How can we help make this class a place where everyone is excited to share their musical compositions?

Sol and Mi Compositions: Star Light Star Bright

Composing Project: *Sol* and *mi* vocal compositions

Preparing the Project:

- Before the project, students should have conscious knowledge of *sol* and *mi*. They should also be able to sing "Star Light Star Bright" without teacher assistance. If *sol* and *mi* are unknown vocabulary, students may use high and low instead and transition to *sol* and *mi* throughout the course of the project.
- **Teaching the Song Through Creative Listening:** Sing the song as students listen and pat a steady beat. Ask questions between each repetition of the song: *What do you notice about this song? Who do you think would sing this? What do you think they were wishing for? What would you wish for?* After several repetitions, students sing the second half of the song on their own. Eventually transition to students singing the whole song without assistance.

CLASS 1

Objective: Students create movements to match the melodic contour of a *sol* and *mi* melody

Assessment:

The student's movements match the melodic contour of the *sol* and *mi* melody	
3	The student's movements match the melodic contour of the *sol* and *mi* melody
1	The student's movements do not match the melodic contour of the *sol* and *mi* melody, or the student does not move

Process:

- Sing the song and pat a steady beat.
- *What would you look like if you were a star?* Take student answers. (We might shimmer with our fingers, we might stand on our tiptoes, we might spin in place etc.)
- Motion for students to sing the song as they show their star movements in place.
- *What would you look like if you were pretending to be a shooting star moving around the room?* Take student answers. (We might move quickly, we might move high to low, etc.)
- Sing the song again. Choose a few students at a time to show their shooting star movements in open space as the rest of the class shows their stationary movements at their spots.
  - **SEL Social Awareness:** *Why is it important to look for open space when we move around the room with our music friends? How does looking for open space keep the other musicians here safe?*
- The students who moved as shooting stars choose the next stars to move around the room. Continue singing the song.
  - **Facilitating Creative Movement:** Young movers are not always ready to move around the room in open space. To facilitate creative locomotor movement, select a small number of students to move

around the room. Gradually add more students when the movers demonstrate they are aware of their physical surroundings as they perform their movements.

- Seated in their spots, ask students to echo your melodic pattern with stationary movements that match the melody's melodic contour. Improvise several *sol mi* examples with varying lengths of rhythms and articulations:

- **An Aural Context:** How many musical and artistic variations of *sol* and *mi* can you create in the four-beat phrase? This echo work creates an aural context for *sol* and *mi* that students will utilize in their melodic creations.

- After several rounds, ask students to notice the two pitches being used in the melodies: high and low. Perform another improvisation and ask students to echo on solfege syllables.
  - **Flexible Levels of Notational Literacy:** Students may aurally identify these pitches as *sol* and *mi*. If *sol* and *mi* are not conscious vocabulary, ask students to echo sing on "high" and "low."
- Invite a student musician to sing a melody instead and have the class echo sing with high and low movements that match the melodic contour.

CLASS 2

Objective: Students create a melody using *sol* and *mi*

Assessment:

The student creates a melody using *sol* and *mi*	
3	The student creates a melody using *sol* and *mi*
1	The student does not create a melody using *sol* and *mi*, or does not participate

Process:

- Lead students in singing the song showing stationary shooting star movements.
- Sing the song again. Choose a few students at a time to show their shooting star movements in open space as the rest of the class shows their stationary movements at their spots.
- As a B section, ask students to echo your melodic pattern with stationary movements. Improvise four *sol* and *mi* examples like in the previous class.
- Ask the students who were moving in open space to come back to the group and tag their movement replacement as the whole class sings the song.
- Perform the song with all students moving in ABA:
  - A: Sing the song and move around in open space
  - B: Stand still and echo sing four *sol* and *mi* patterns in a row
  - A: Sing the song and move around in open space

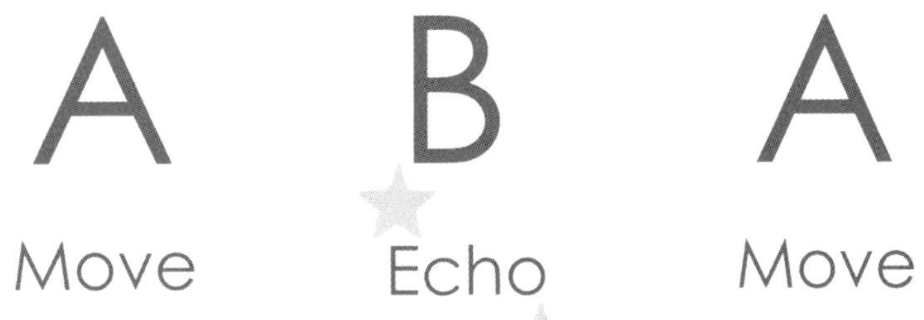

- After several rounds, invite a student musician to sing the B section melodies and have the class echo sing with movements.
- Ask the class to sing the song as they move back to their spots.
- In their spots, ask students to turn to their shoulder partner and create their own *sol* and *mi* melody using solfege syllables and movement. Both partners should be able to sing the melody. Let students know they'll have the opportunity to share their ideas in a few moments.
  - **Flexible Levels of Notational Literacy:** If students do not yet have conscious knowledge of *sol* and *mi*, ask them to use "high" and "low" with high and low hand signs instead.
- Before asking students to share their ideas, help them check their work:
  - We can both sing the melody
  - We use solfege (or "high" "low") and and movement
- Walk around the room as students work and listen to their melodies.
  - If students' melodies start to sound too similar to each other, consider repeating the *sol* and *mi* echo activity from earlier. Take care that the melodies you provide show many *sol* and *mi* possibilities for students to aurally experience.
- Invite student pairs to teach their melodic ideas to the class. The rest of the class echoes.
  - **SEL Responsible Decision-Making:** Musicians can make mistakes! Help students problem-solve as creative performers by making a plan for what to do if they make a mistake when sharing their melody idea.
- After a few moments, choose one melody from students to write on the board using a five-line staff. Students help by showing the placement of the pitches using a hand staff. Review steps and skips on the staff as necessary.
  - **Flexible Levels of Notational Literacy:** If students do not have conscious knowledge of *sol* and *mi*, use graphic notation instead of writing the melody on the five-line staff. Then, label the two pitches as *sol* and *mi* and show their placement on the staff.

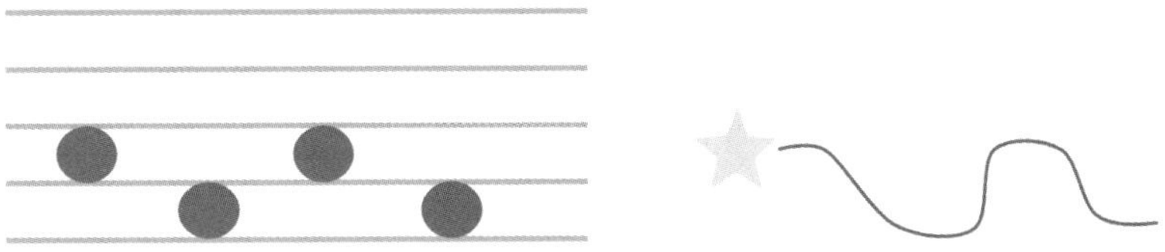

CLASS 3

Objective: Students notate their *sol* and *mi* composition

Assessment:

Composition: The student notates their *sol* and *mi* composition	
3	The student notates their composed *sol* and *mi* melody
1	The student does not notate their composed *sol* and *mi* melody
Notation: The student notates their *sol* and *mi* composition on the five line staff	
4	The student notates their entire *sol* and *mi* composition accurately on the five line staff; all noteheads are written clearly on the appropriate spaces
3	The student notates their *sol* and *mi* composition on the five line staff; note heads are written approximately on the appropriate spaces
2	The student notates their composition on the five line staff; note heads are written inaccurately
1	The student writes illegibly, or does not write

Materials: "Shooting Star" composition worksheet

- Briefly review the ABA movement activity from the previous class:
    - A: Sing the song and move around in open space
    - B: Stand still and echo sing four *sol* and *mi* patterns in a row
    - A: Sing the song and move around in open space

- With students seated, review the placement of *sol* and *mi* on the staff.
- Tell students they'll write down their own melodies to share with other friends and show an example of a completed version of the worksheet. Students may choose to write their composition in solfege or graphic notation first. After it's written with solfege or graphic notation, students write their melody on the staff.

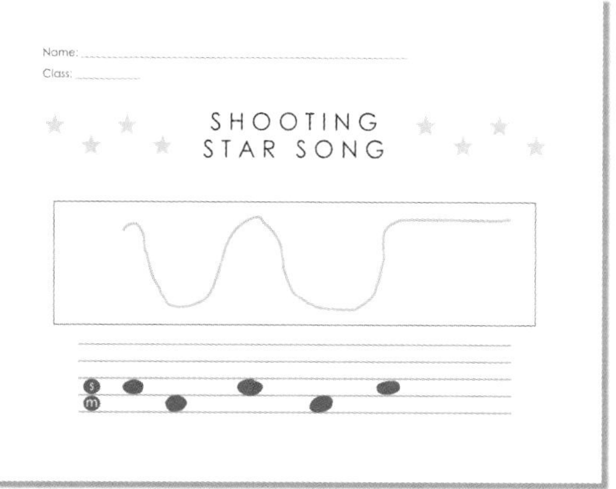

- Ask students to turn to a shoulder partner and create a new melody using *sol* and *mi* by singing and signing solfege. Tell students they should check their work before writing down their melody idea using the checks from last class. After they're done writing, they should check to see if their melody matches what they wrote.

> **SEL Self-Management:** What should students do if they have a question while they're working? What steps should they walk through to problem-solve on their own? When is it appropriate for them to ask you for help?

- As students work, walk around the room and pass out the worksheets and pencils.
- When students have a melody they like and after they've checked their work, they write down their composition.
- Walk around as students work on their compositions. Encourage students to double-check their work by making sure the melody they hear in their head matches the melody they wrote. If there is a discrepancy, would they like to change their melody to match the notation, or the notation to match the melody? Double-check to make sure both worksheets have the same melody written down.
- After a few moments, ask student groups to pair with another student group. Each pair takes turns teaching their song to their classmates.
- Ask students to write their names at the top of the paper and point to them.
- Students sing "Star Light Star Bright" as they hold their paper in the air and the teacher collects them.

COMPOSITION: UPPER ELEMENTARY

Taka-di Class Composition: Skipping Rope Song

English Jump-Rope Game

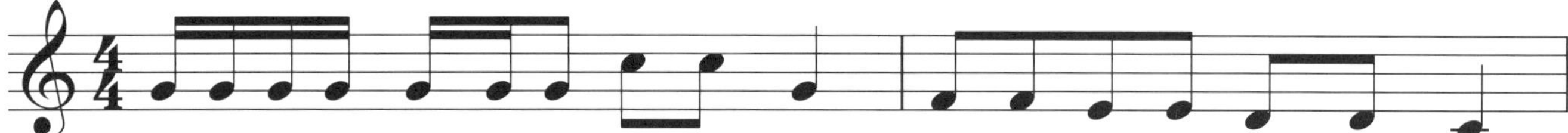

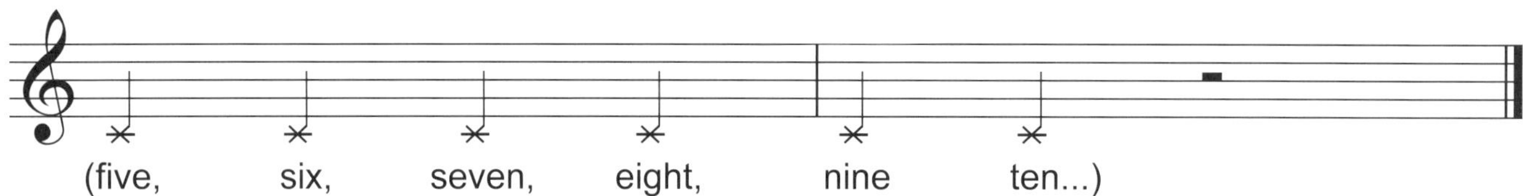

Game: Two students hold a jump rope. A few students at a time line up behind the rope, ready to jump in. The class sings the song and sings the first student's name to jump in the rope. At the end of the song, continue counting to see how many jumps the student can do. Repeat the game calling in the next student.

Composing Project: Create a class composition using *taka-di*

Preparing the Project:

- Before the project, students should have conscious knowledge of steady beat, rhythm, rhythm vs beat, quarter notes, eighth notes, quarter rest, *takadimi*, *ta-dimi*, and *taka-di*. If *taka-di* is not a known element, students may transition to using it throughout the course of the project. Students should also be able to sing the song and play the game to "Skipping Rope Song" without teacher assistance.
- **Teaching the Song Through Creative Listening:** Lead students in performing an ostinato on body percussion of their choice as they listen to the song:

Ask questions between repetitions of the song (*What was the postman delivering? What do you think the letters said? Was Ella expecting the letters or were they a surprise? Who were they from?*) Add the game. Students perform the ostinato and sing the second half of the song ("Up jumps __ student name__ to open the door, one letter two letters three letters four"). Eventually transition to students singing the entire song without assistance.

CLASS 1

Objective: Students pat taka-di in the rhythm of the song

Assessment:

The student pats *taka-di* in the rhythm of the song	
4	The student pats *taka-di* in the rhythm of the song with precise rhythmic accuracy throughout the entire performance
3	The student pats *taka-di* in the rhythm of the song accurately
2	The student pats *taka-di* in the rhythm of the song with inaccuracies throughout much of the performance
1	The student incorrectly pats taka-di in the rhythm of the song, or does not participate

Materials: Jump rope

Process:

- Lead students in singing and play the game. Listen to students singing the song without assistance.
- Add an ostinato on body percussion of students' choice and play four times in a row:

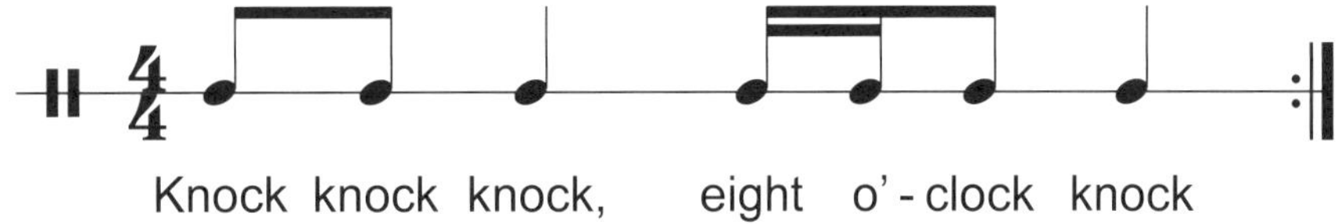

- After practicing the ostinato, lead students in patting the rhythm of the song.
  - **Rhythm Performance:** When students play quick, short rhythms like those in this song, they should keep the motion of their hands small. Playing quietly will help students be more articulate. This is preparation for playing hand drums in another class.
- Ask students to choose if they'll play the ostinato or pat the rhythm of the song and give a thumbs up when they have their choice.
- Perform the song, then experiment with more ostinato options:
- *What would the postman's knocks sound like if the postman were in a hurry and was knocking with short fast rhythms?* Lead a new ostinato:

- Divide the class in half. One half performs the ostinato and the other pats the rhythm of the song.
- Add another ostinato option: *What if the postman didn't have coffee that day and their knock had lots of space between the rhythms?* Lead a new ostinato:

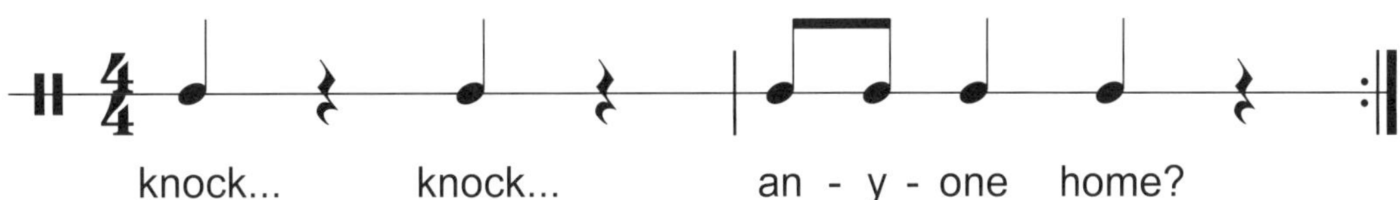

- Divide the class in half. One half performs the ostinato and the other pats the rhythm of the song.
- Ask students to notice that each ostinato has a rhythm that can be repeated. Tell students they'll create ostinato patterns and share them with the class in a few minutes.

- Ask students to get into groups between two and four and develop an ostinato. The ostinato can be busy, calm, or in-between. All members of the group should be able to play the ostinato four times in a row.
    - **SEL Social Awareness:** *What happens if there are too many people in one group? How should we navigate who stays in the group and who finds a new group? What can the rest of the class do to make our groups welcoming for someone looking for a new group to join?*
- Optional: As students work, walk around the room and pass out rhythm sticks so students can perform their ostinato patterns on the floor.
- After a few moments, check in with the class to see how much longer they need to work. Remind students that all members of the group should be able to play the ostinato four times.
- Do a whole-class run through. Listen to students sing the song and observe all groups performing their ostinati.
- Ask student volunteers to share as the rest of the class plays the rhythm of the song. When the group is done performing, take feedback from the class. The group who just performed calls on the next student group to share.
    - **SEL Relationship Skills:** What does active listening look like for the audience? What type of body language and musical engagement will support the performers?

CLASS 2

Objective: Students improvise with *taka-di*

Assessment:

The student improvises using *taka-di*	
3	The student improvises using *taka-di*
1	The student does not improvise with *taka-di*, or does not improvise

Materials: Jump rope

Process:

- Lead students in singing and play the game. Listen to students singing the song without assistance.
- Add an ostinato on body percussion of students' choice:

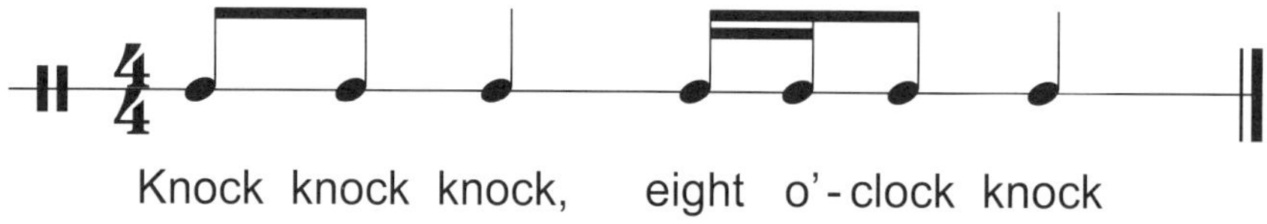

Students choose if they'll perform the ostinato or play the rhythm of the song, then perform their choice.

- *Let's imagine we're reading a letter and it sounds like this:* (Read the following text rapidly, without pausing for a breath.) *Earlyinthemorningateight-o'-clockyoucanhearthepostman'sknockupjumpsellatoopenthedooronelettertwoletteresthreelettersfour.*
- *Notice that the letter doesn't have anywhere for us to breathe when we read it! When we compose music, it can be a good idea to include places where there are busy rhythms and places there are calm rhythms. Let's practice that together.*
- Take student suggestions for a calm eight-beat rhythm.
    - **Example:**

- Ask half the class to play the calm rhythm as an ostinato with the rest of the class patting the rhythm of the words to "Skipping Rope Song."
- If students agree to the use of the pattern as the calm rhythm, ask a student volunteer to write it on the board.
- In between playing the calm rhythm, ask students to improvise eight-beat rhythms that are busy. Play a few examples as students perform a steady beat, such as:

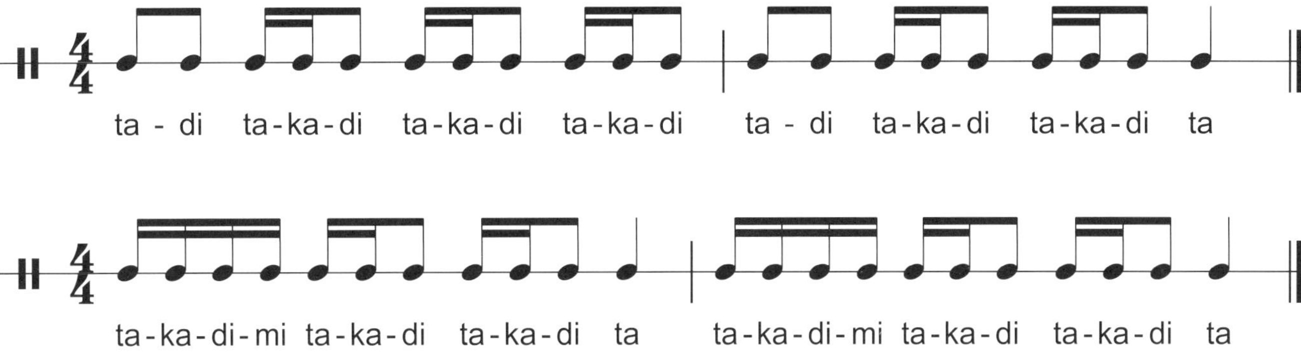

- Follow the outline on the board for playing the calm rhythm and improvising the busy rhythm. Encourage students to improvise different rhythms both times.

I If students struggle to follow the order on the board, do a "dry run" to map out the form without improvisation. During the improvised section, have all students speak the text together instead of improvising:

- When students are ready, move on to the next activity.

I **Note:** This class composition will be different in every class, since students suggest their own order for a calm rhythm and they improvise their own busy rhythms.

- Play the rhythm of the song as the A section.
- As the B section, ask students to walk around the room in open space as they play the calm rhythm and to stop moving to improvise the busy rhythms. Listen and observe as students improvise and move as the B section.

I **Scaffolding Improvisation:** If students struggle to know when to stop improvising, continue using the movement activity but ask students to play the calm rhythm and whisper the placeholder text ("make it up make it up...") instead of playing their improvisation.

- After practicing several options for improvisation, ask students to use *taka-di* in their busy rhythm.

- **Flexible Levels of Notational Literacy:** If *taka-di* is a new rhythmic element for students, ask them to notice the long and short sounds in "early in the morning at eight o'-clock." Ask students to notice that beat two of the phrase has two short sounds and one long sound on one beat (the words, "morning at"). Label this as *taka-di*.

- Repeat the activity, singing the song as the A section and performing busy and calm rhythms as the B section.
- After the improvisation, ask students if they used *taka-di* in their improvisation. Students give a thumbs up if they did, a thumbs down if they did not, and a sideways thumb if they don't know.

CLASS 3

Objective: Students perform a class composition using *taka-di*

Assessment:

The student performs a class composition using *taka-di*	
3	The student performs a class composition using *taka-di*
1	The student does not perform a class composition using *taka-di*
The student legibly notates *taka-di* in an eight-beat rhythmic composition	
3	The student legibly notates *taka-di* in an eight-beat rhythmic composition
2	The student notates *taka-di* in an eight-beat rhythmic composition with approximate notation
1	The student notates *taka-di* in an eight-beat rhythmic composition inaccurately, or does not include *taka-di*

Materials: Jump rope, "Skipping Rope" rhythm composition worksheet; tubanos (enough for students to share with a partner)

Process:

- Lead students in singing and play the game.
- Review the improvisation activity from last class: Play the rhythm of the song as the A section. As the B section, ask students to walk around the room in open space as they play the calm rhythm and to stop moving to improvise the busy rhythms. Listen and observe as students improvise and move as the B section.
  - Recall the calm rhythm from last class, or develop a new one and write it on the board.

- After the activity, ask students to turn to a partner and work together to develop an eight-beat rhythm that incorporates *taka-di*. Give students time to work on their rhythm and preserve through memorization. Both partners should be able to perform the rhythm on body percussion two times in a row.
  - **SEL Relationship Skills:** How do musicians collaborate to create something new? Students might recall one of their improvisations and take turns teaching it to their partner. The pair might choose one of their rhythms to use. Students might also find a way to combine their rhythms to create a full eight-beat phrase. Alternatively, students might develop an entirely new rhythm from scratch.
- As students work, walk around the room passing out rhythm composition papers and pencils. Let students know they'll write the rhythms later. For now, they're preserving their composition through memorization.

- When students show that they're ready, do a whole-class runthrough of student-created rhythms. Listen for students starting and stopping together after eight beats.
- Ask students if their composition uses *taka-di*. Students give a thumbs up if it does, a thumbs down if it does not, and a sideways thumb if they don't know.
  - Use this time to observe which groups might need more assistance in the development of their rhythm. Check in with these groups as the class notates their composition.
- Ask students to write down their eight-beat rhythm composition. Let students know that the rest of the class will read their rhythm, so they should check that it's written neatly.
  - **Flexible Levels of Notational Literacy:** If *taka-di* is a new element, show the notation on the board. Guide the notation of a sample student composition on the board as an example.

Write your eight-beat rhythm using taka-di in the box below. Write your names on the back of the paper.

Write your eight-beat rhythm using taka-di in the box below. Write your names on the back of the paper.

- When students have their rhythms written down, create a circle of tubanos with one partner on the inside and the other on the outside. The partner on the outside holds the rhythm card the pair just composed.

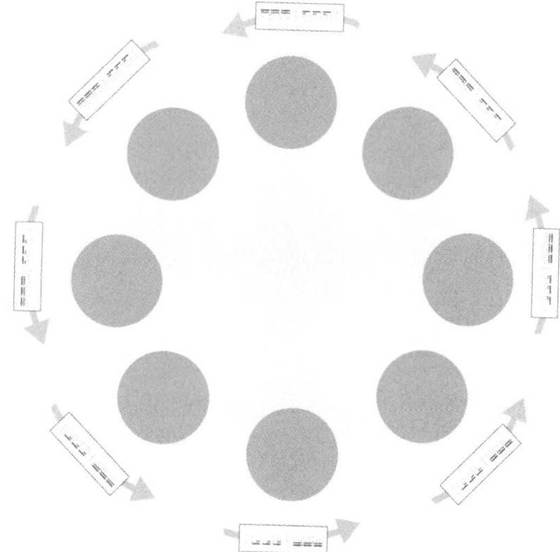

- Tell students that just like the body percussion improvisation activity from earlier, the students on the outside of the circle will move during the calm rhythms and stand still during the busy rhythms. During the calm rhythm, students on the outside step to the right so they are standing in front of a new partner. After the calm rhythm, the students on the right stand still so their new partner can sight-read the rhythm they are holding up. Students will continue around the circle, moving and pausing for classmates to read.

- After a few rounds, switch jobs so the inside and outside circles switch places.
- With written permission from administration and student guardians, preserve the full class composition by videoing or recording audio.

Extension:

- Create two circles of tubanos and perform the composition in a round.

Question-and-Answer Form Compositions: Rocky Mountain

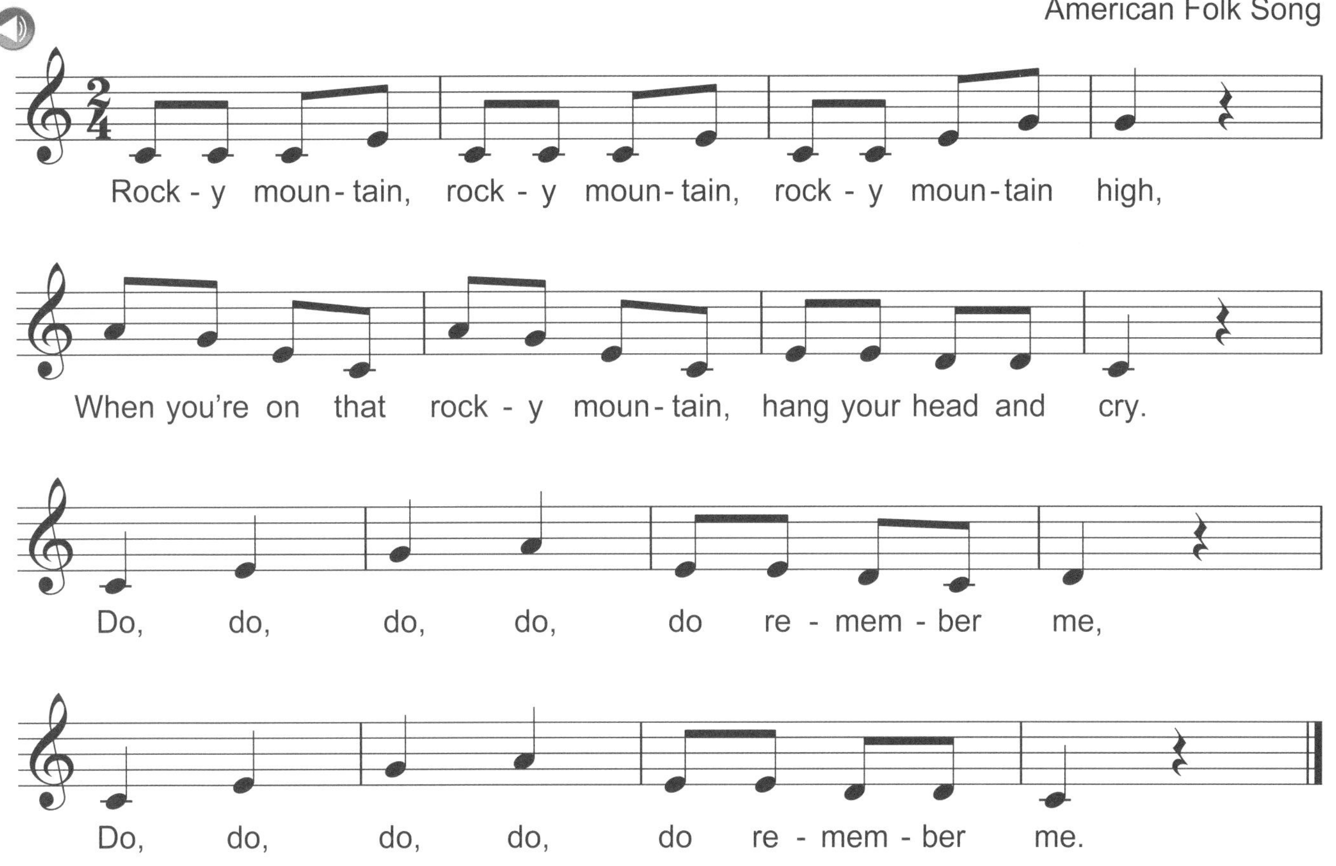

Composing Project: Composing in question-and-answer form

Preparing the Project:

- Before the project, students should have conscious knowledge of *do, re, mi, sol,* and *la*. Students should also be able to sing the song without teacher assistance.
- **Teaching the Song:** Stand in a circle. Lead students in stepping a steady beat eight counts in one direction, then eight counts in another direction throughout the song.

CLASS 1

Objective: Students sing chord roots (*do* and *sol*) to "Rocky Mountain"

Assessment:

Students sing chord roots (*do* and *sol*) to "Rocky Mountain"	
4	The student sings chord roots (*do* and *sol*) to "Rocky Mountain" with complete pitch accuracy throughout the entire performance
3	The student sings chord roots (*do* and *sol*) to "Rocky Mountain"
2	The students sing chord roots (*do* and *sol*) to "Rocky Mountain" with approximate pitch, following the melodic contour
1	Student inaccurately sings chord roots (*do* and *sol*) to "Rocky Mountain," or does not sing

Process:

- Lead students in singing the song while stepping around the room in open space. As students move, add a harmonic accompaniment through singing or with a barred instrument.

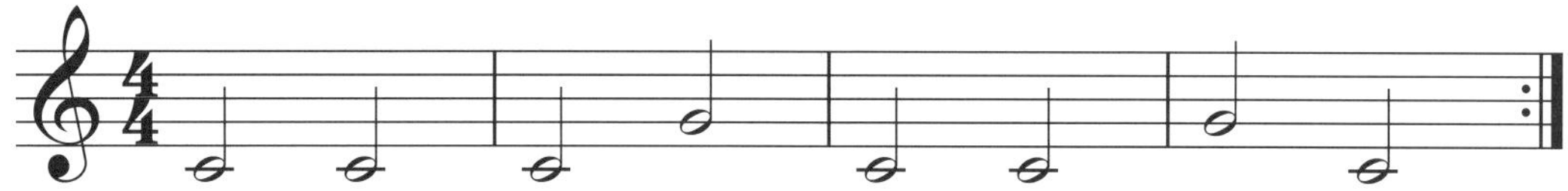

- Listen for students matching pitch and singing without assistance.
- Analyze the cadence at the end of the first line: *Do we end on* do *or* sol? (*Sol.*) *Is* sol *our "home" note or the "away" note?* (Away.) *How is that different from the second line?* (The second line ends on *do*, the "home" note.)
- With a partner, ask students to create a high shape, like they're standing at the top of a mountain, and a low shape like they're standing at the base of a mountain. Tell students their shapes will be safe and musical.
  - **SEL Relationship Skills:** What should a student do if their partner wants to create a shape that is not safe or musical? Help students with language that is assertive when they encounter negative social pressure.
- Ask students to sing the first half of the song while walking in open space with a partner. Freeze at the end of the first phrase on the high shape. Freeze at the end of the second phrase on the low shape.
- Show the notation of the chord roots on the board in mountain shapes.

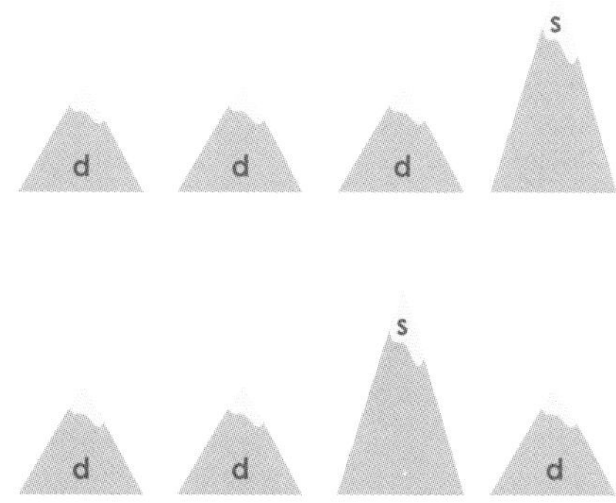

- Seated, students sing the first half of the song while the teacher sings the chord roots and shows the solfege hand signs.
- Students choose if they'll sing and sign with solfege hand signs or with their mountain movements they just created and give a thumbs up when they have their choice.
- Students sing the chord roots without the teacher's assistance.
- Students sing the chord roots with their choice of solfege hand signs or mountain movements while the teacher sings the first half of the song.
- Choose a few student volunteers to sing the first half of the song while stepping in open space. The rest of the class sings the chord roots with their mountain shapes. As students sing, the teacher uses a barred instrument and improvises in question-and-answer form, ending the first phrase on *sol* and the ending phrase on *do*.

CLASS 2

Objective: Students improvise a melodic question ending on dominant and an answer ending on tonic

Assessment:

The student improvises a melodic question ending on dominant and an answer ending on tonic	
3	The student improvises a melodic question ending on dominant and an answer ending on tonic
1	The student improvises a melodic question that does not end on dominant, and / or the student improvises a melodic answer that does not end on tonic

Materials: Barred instruments set up in C pentatonic. (If the instrumentation is available, students may each play their own barred instrument. If not, students will share instruments and play by tapping their fingers on the bars.)

Process:

- With their partner from last class or with a new partner, ask students to create a high shape and a low shape.
- Lead students in checking their work with a whole-class run through: Lead students in singing the song while walking in open space with their partner. Freeze at the end of the first phrase on the high shape. Freeze at the end of the second phrase on the low shape.
- Tell students this is the A section.
- *How many steady beats are in the first phrase?* Students inner hear and share their answer (eight beats). *How many steady beats are in the second phrase?* Students inner hear the song and share their answer (eight beats).
- The teacher improvises eight beats on body percussion. Students respond with their own eight-beat improvisation on body percussion.
- Repeat the activity, but ask students to stand still when they listen to the teacher's improvisation and move when they improvise their response.
- Ask students to improvise their answer on body percussion as they move to a barred instrument with their partner.
  - If the instrumentation is available, students may each play their own barred instrument. If not, two students will share an instrument.
- With two musicians at a barred instrument, invite students to experiment with the sounds they can make moving up and down their instrument like a mountain. Ask students to figure out where *do*, *re*, *mi*, *sol*, and *la* live on the barred instrument if C is *do*.
  - **Exploration:** This is the time for students to play around. For our purposes, any exploratory sounds they make that are safe and musical are appropriate. If students are new to exploratory play on the instruments, take a few moments to discuss expectations and procedures such as rest position and playing technique.
- After both partners have had a turn at the barred instruments, ask them to work together to figure out the chord roots on the barred instrument.

- Play the chord roots together as an ensemble. The partner without mallets sings on solfege to help the partner with mallets. Switch jobs and repeat the activity.
- *Let's add the B section. This time please play your answer on* do *(C) if you have the mallets. Continue playing your answer on body percussion if you do not have the mallets right now.*
- Sing the A section of the song ("Rocky mountain rocky mountain"). Then, the teacher improvises eight beats on a barred instrument, starting on *do* (C) and ending on *sol* (G). Students play their own rhythmic response on *do* (stay on C the whole time).
  - **Scaffolding:** If you notice students having a hard time recognizing when to stop playing, you may move back to improvising with body percussion and continue with the rest of the barred instrument activities in another class.
- Ask students to observe that there are two pentatonic sets on the instrument: one low and one high. Ask students to choose if they'll use the low or high set for their improvisation.
- The teacher plays the question using the full pentatone and ending on *sol* (G). Students play their answers using the full pentatone, ending on *do* (C). Students without mallets improvise their answers on body percussion. Switch jobs.
- Invite students to play the question using the pentatone, ending on G. Students without mallets improvise their answers on body percussion, ending with a high level like a snap or clap. The teacher responds with an answer ending on C. Switch jobs.
- Sing the A section of the song ("Rocky mountain rocky mountain"). Then, one partner plays the first eight beats, ending on *sol*, and the other plays the second eight beats, ending on *do*.
  - If students are sharing an instrument, one student plays on the lower octave while the partner plays the higher octave. Both students tap the bars if mallets for every student are unavailable.

CLASS 3

Objective: Students notate their composition

Assessment:

The student notates their melodic composition	
3	The student notates their melodic composition
1	The student does not notate their melodic composition

Materials: Barred instruments set up in C pentatonic (enough for students to share with a partner), "Rocky Mountain" composition worksheet, pencils

Process:

- Review the improvisation activity from the previous class. Students sit behind a barred instrument with a partner. Sing the A section of the song ("Rocky mountain rocky mountain"). Then, as a B section one partner plays the first eight beats, ending on *sol*, and the other plays the second eight beats, ending on *do*.
    - If students are sharing an instrument, one student plays on the lower octave while the partner plays the higher octave. Both students tap the bars if mallets for every student are unavailable. If the instrumentation is available, students may each play their own barred instrument.
- After a while, ask partners to choose their favorite melodies they've created. Students work together to each play their combined melodies, with the first eight-beat phrase ending on *sol* and the second eight-beat phrase ending on *do*.
- Challenge students to solidify their melodies by playing them four times in a row.
- *How many beats are in the first phrase?* (Eight.) *How many beats are in the second phrase?* (Eight.)
- Show an example of a composition worksheet that is in progress (notated with solfege, graphic notation, or letter names) and a composition worksheet that is complete (transferred to the five-line staff).

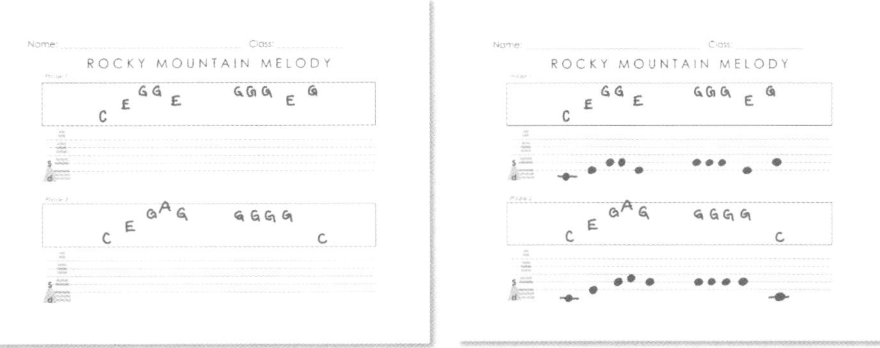

- Let students know that both partners will have their own notation sheet, and their melodies should match. They may preserve their melodies in graphic notation, solfege syllables, or letter names before transferring the melodies to the staff. They do not need to write their rhythms. In the next class they will share their compositions with their partner in a small group. Ask students for questions they have about the process.
    - **SEL Self-Awareness:** *Musicians use many different systems of notation to share their ideas. What kind of notation system makes the most sense to you? What will be the most meaningful way for you to notate your composition? This is something you'll write down today and use in the next class, so take care that you notate your melody in a way you'll remember.*
- Students work together to solidify their melodies. Both partners should be able to play the first eight beats ending on *sol* and the last eight beats ending on *do*. Challenge students to play their melodies four times in a row to memorize them before writing them down.
- As students play their melodies four times in a row, pass out the composition worksheets and pencils.
- Students may choose to write their composition in letter names, solfege, or graphic notation first. After it's written with letter names, solfege, or graphic notation, students write their melody on the staff.
- **Applying Qualitative Assessment Data:** As students work, walk around the room and observe. What do students need assistance with before moving on? What do students' notation choices show about their understanding of melodic contour? Use this information to guide future instruction.
- Students practice their melody to make sure the sounds they hear in their heads match the notation on the page. Students should also check that both partners are playing the same melody, and that the first phrase ends on *sol* and the second phrase ends on *do*.
- Toward the end of the lesson segment, give students a few moments to organize their thinking and make notes on the back of the worksheet.

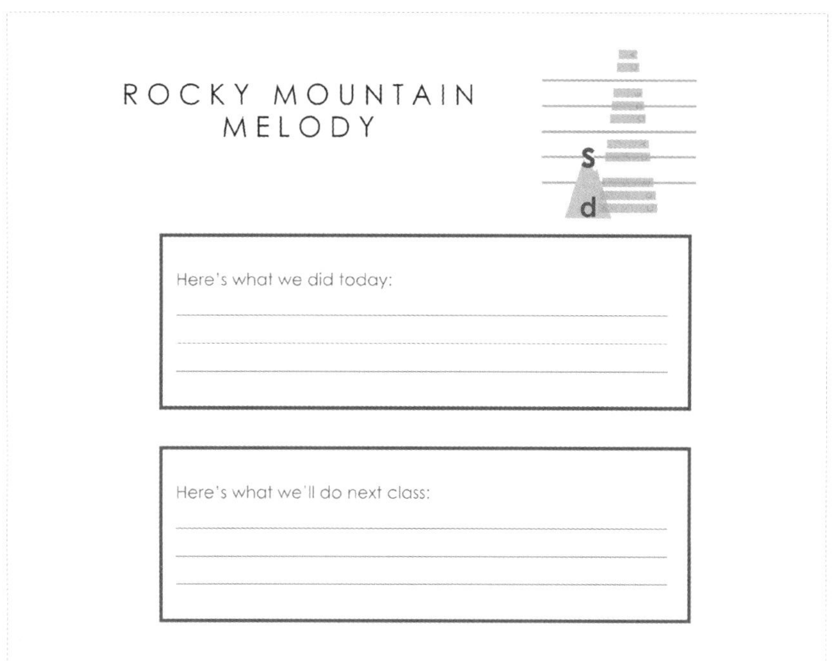

- **SEL Self-Management:** Students take time to reflect on their progress during class and map their goals for next time. Both students complete the prompts about what they did in class, and what the next steps are. Example statements might be: "Today we played our song and wrote it down with letter names. Next class we'll check to make sure we still like this melody, and then write it on the five-line staff. Hopefully we can practice it before we share it with the class."

CLASS 4

Objective: Students notate and perform their compositions

Assessment:

Notation: The student notates their melodic composition in question-and-answer form, ending the first phrase on *sol* (G) and the second phrase on *do* (C).	
3	The student notates their melodic composition in question-and-answer form, ending the first phrase on *sol* (G) and the second phrase on *do* (C).
2	The student notates their melodic composition without question-and-answer form, ending the first phrase on a pitch other than *sol* (G) and the second phrase on a pitch other than *do* (C).
1	The student does not notate their melodic composition, or writes illegibly
Performance: The student performs their melodic composition	
4	The student performs their composition with complete accuracy throughout the entire performance, ending the first phrase on *sol* and the second phrase on *do*.
3	The student performs their composition with accuracy throughout most of the performance, with a few minor variations from the notation.
2	The student performs their composition with multiple inaccuracies from the written notation
1	The student does not perform their composition

Materials: Barred instruments set up in C pentatonic (enough for students to share with a partner), "Rocky Mountain" composition worksheet, pencils

Process:

- Give students a few moments to practice their composition and make any adjustments they need so that the notation reflects their composition. Tell students that in a few moments, they'll share their compositions in a small group. The partners will play their melodies while the other group members sing chord roots.

- As students work, walk around the room. Check in with students to see if they're ready to share their composition.
  - **SEL Self-Management:** When you check in with students, ask them how many more minutes their group needs to be ready to share their composition.
- *How will we know we've done a good job in our composition sharing?* Work together as a class to create a small checklist (three to five items) of criteria. Write students' assessment criteria on the board.
  - Sample criteria might be:
    We play our compositions together
    The notation of the song matches what we play
    The group sings chord roots
- Do a whole-class practice of student compositions and a whole-class practice of singing chord roots. Ask students if they're ready to share or if they would prefer another round of practice.
  - **SEL Responsible Decision-Making:** *It's normal for musicians to make mistakes when they perform for an audience! If you're performing for your group and you or your partner makes a mistake, what should you do?*
- Ask students to take their instruments and combine with another set of partners to make a small group of four.
  - If students have been sharing instruments, each partner will now have their own instrument to play when the partner groups are combined. Give students a few moments to turn their mallets around and practice their composition on the new instrument before sharing with the group.
- The other students in the group sing chord roots to accompany the student composers.
- The composers who shared turn their papers and instruments around, and teach their composition to the other musicians in the group using a combination of rote teaching and notation. After a few moments, ask the group to give feedback and positive observations about the composition.
  - Depending on the size of your room, you might choose for students to turn their mallets around to lower the volume level.
- Repeat the activity with the other pair of composers in the group.

Extensions:

- **Composition Extensions:** Could student compositions work in a round? Could one of the compositions work as a partner melody with the main song, or as a partner melody with another composition?
- **Ensemble:** Put the composition in context with the song. During the A section, some students move with mountain shapes while others sing the song. Transfer the chord roots to a bass xylophone. Choose a few students to perform their compositions as a B section.
- **Sharing:** Consider videoing student compositions after getting written consent from administration and students' guardians. These compositions and the notation of the compositions might be shared on the school website or through another parent communication platform. The notation of the compositions can also make an informative hallway display.